MASTER THE™ CLEP®

Introductory Sociology Exam

PETERSON'S®

About Peterson's®

Peterson's has been your trusted educational publisher for more than 50 years. It's a milestone we're quite proud of as we continue to offer the most accurate, dependable, high-quality educational content in the field, providing you with everything you need to succeed. No matter where you are on your academic or professional path, you can rely on Peterson's for its books, videos, online information, expert test-prep tools, the most up-to-date education exploration data, and the highest quality career success resources—everything you need to achieve your education goals. For our complete line of products, visit **www.petersons.com**.

For more information, contact Peterson's, 4380 S. Syracuse St., Suite 200, Denver, CO 80237; 800-338-3282, ext. 54229; or visit us online at **www.petersons.com**.

Contents

Before You Begin

OVERVIEW
- Why You Should Use This Book
- How This Book Is Organized
- Peterson's Publications
- Give Us Your Feedback

WHY YOU SHOULD USE THIS BOOK

Peterson's *Master the™ CLEP® Introductory Sociology Exam* is designed by test experts and educators to fully prepare you for test-day success. This helpful guide includes the following:

- **Essential test information:** We take the stress out of planning for a CLEP exam by providing all the information you'll need to know before the big day in one place—including how to register, where to go, and what to bring on the day of the exam.
- **Comprehensive coverage of the exam format:** After using this book, you'll know the structure and format of the CLEP Introductory Sociology exam from start to finish.
- **Expert tips, advice, and strategies:** Our test-prep professionals are veteran educators who know what it takes to prepare well for CLEP exams—you'll get expert tools and strategies that have proven to be effective on exam day, giving you the confidence to get the credit you deserve. Consider this your inside edge as you jump-start your education or career advancement journey.
- **Test topic review:** You'll get a review of the concepts presented in each exam domain and advice on creating an effective study plan for reaching your goal score. Not only will there be no surprises on test day, but you'll also have the confidence that comes with being thoroughly prepared.
- **Diagnostic and practice tests to support your study plan:** Take a diagnostic test to help you determine your strengths and weaknesses and target your study time effectively. Then, build your confidence

with Readiness Check reviews and Test Yourself practice questions at the end of each chapter. When you're close to test day, take the practice test to gauge your progress and determine what to study in your final review.

Peterson's *Master the™ CLEP° Introductory Sociology Exam* is an excellent review tool to prepare you for the exam, but it is not designed to teach you the subjects covered on the exam—all CLEP exams are intended for students who have at least some working knowledge of a topic rather than complete beginners. Before signing up to take any CLEP exam, be sure to review the appropriate "Resource Guide and Sample Questions" PDF on the College Board CLEP website (**https://clep.collegeboard.org**) to verify your familiarity with the subjects and terminology presented in the outline. That said, if you are new to the topic of sociology and nonetheless want to try to pass the exam, this book can serve as a great overview of the topics you'll need to dive into deeper as you prepare.

We know that doing well on the CLEP exam is important, and we're here to help you through every step of your journey. Consider this book your test-prep compass—it will guide you through preparing for your CLEP exam and get you started earning your well-deserved college credits.

HOW THIS BOOK IS ORGANIZED

Peterson's *Master the™ CLEP° Introductory Sociology Exam* provides information about the exam, tips and strategies for exam day, a diagnostic test, subject-matter review, and a practice test.

- **CLEP exam overview:** Chapter 1 tells you all you need to know about CLEP exams. You'll learn about the purpose of the exams, how to register, what to do on test day, and more. We've also included a specific breakdown of what you can expect to see on the CLEP Introductory Sociology exam.
- **Tips and strategies:** Chapter 2 covers a variety of study strategies and test-taking tips. We encourage you to look over this chapter periodically throughout your study to remind yourself of these tips and strategies throughout your preparation process.
- **Diagnostic test:** The diagnostic test (Chapter 3) consists of 25 multiple-choice questions (a quarter of the length of the full CLEP exam), followed by an answer key and detailed answer explanations. This test is designed to measure your current knowledge.

- **Diagnostic test evaluation:** These scoring charts, examples, and instructions are designed to help you identify the areas you need to focus on based on your test results and serve as the starting point as you build a study plan to achieve your target score.
- **Sociology content review:** Each of the five content review chapters (Chapters 4–8) centers on one of the main scoring categories of the CLEP Introductory Sociology exam, providing a general overview of the sociology subjects, topics, and terminology covered in the exam.
- **Bold key terms:** The **bold key terms** throughout identify sociology-specific names, concepts, and terminology. If a term is unfamiliar, look up how it is used in the context of the social sciences and add it to your study list.
- **Readiness Checks:** Readiness Checks near the end of each content review chapter (Chapters 4–8) feature questions about key concepts that you need to understand for each scoring category on the exam. While these don't cover every single question that might come up, they are a useful way to evaluate your knowledge about the main topic.
- **Test Yourself practice questions:** The Test Yourself sections at the end of each content review chapter (Chapters 4–8) consist of five practice questions from the sociology category covered in that chapter. Use the Test Yourself questions alongside the Readiness Checks to evaluate your knowledge.
- **Practice Test:** The practice test (Chapter 9) consists of 50 multiple-choice questions (half the length of the full CLEP exam), followed by an answer key and detailed answer explanations. This test is designed to measure your progress after studying, but you can take it whenever it suits your study needs.

We recommend starting with the test overview in Chapter 1 and the tips and strategies in Chapter 2. Then, move on to the diagnostic test in Chapter 3. The diagnostic test is designed to help you figure out what you already know and what you need to study. It contains 25 multiple-choice questions like the ones found on the CLEP exam, and they should provide you with a good idea of what to expect and how much you need to study before the official exam.

Once you take the diagnostic test (Chapter 3), check your answers to see how you did. Read the brief answer explanations to see why a specific answer is correct, and in many cases, why other options are incorrect. Use the scoring and evaluation charts to identify the categories of questions you missed so that you can spend your study time reviewing the information that will help you the most. As with any exam, knowing your strengths and areas for improvement greatly improves your chances of success. The sections following the diagnostic test will help you evaluate your results and create a study plan tailored to your specific needs.

Each of the five content review chapters (Chapters 4–8) addresses one of the five categories covered in the CLEP Introductory Sociology exam: institutions, social patterns, social processes, social stratification, and the sociological perspective. Each of these chapters summarizes the category and various subtopics within that category. The order of the content review chapters in this book follows the order of the CLEP test itself, but you may prefer to read them in a different order; for example, you might begin with Chapter 8 since it covers the history of sociology and the methods used in the field. As you read these chapters, some of the information may be familiar, but take note of anything unfamiliar so that you can adequately prepare to understand the concepts as well as someone who has completed a semester-long course in sociology.

After studying the topics covered on the exam, you should be ready to take the practice test. Revisit Chapter 2 after you review the content chapters to remind yourself of the tips and strategies you want to use. We recommend taking the practice test toward the end of your studying to see how much you've improved since the diagnostic test and to identify any areas you may need to prioritize during your final review. The practice test consists of 50 multiple-choice questions (half the length of the full CLEP exam) that reflect the distribution of question types and categories in the official exam. Be sure to read the answer explanations following the test for additional information and details, even if you answered a question correctly. The 100 questions you'll find throughout this book—in the diagnostic test, end-of-chapter Test Yourself sections, and the practice test—amount to a full-length exam. For additional test prep, including full-length practice tests and videos and interactives to support your study, visit **www.petersons.com/testprep/ product/clep-practice-tests-introductory-sociology**.

PETERSON'S PUBLICATIONS

Peterson's publishes a full line of books—career preparation, education exploration, test prep, study skills, and financial aid. You'll find Peterson's titles available for purchase at major retailers or online at **www.petersons.com**. Sign up for one of our online subscription plans and you'll have access to our entire test-prep catalog of more than 150 exams *plus* instructional videos, flash cards, interactive quizzes, and more! Our subscription plans allow you to study at your own pace.

GIVE US YOUR FEEDBACK

Peterson's publications can be found at your local bookstores and libraries, high school guidance offices, college libraries and career centers, and at **www.petersonsbooks.com**. Peterson's books are now also available as ebooks.

We welcome any comments or suggestions you may have—your feedback will help us make educational dreams possible for you and others like you.

Good luck!

Chapter 1

All about the CLEP Introductory Sociology Exam

OVERVIEW
- What Is CLEP?
- Why Take a CLEP Exam?
- How Does CLEP Work?
- CLEP Test Centers
- How to Register for a CLEP Exam
- How to Prepare for a CLEP Exam
- Test Day
- Introductory Sociology Exam Overview

WHAT IS CLEP?

The College-Level Examination Program (CLEP) provides an opportunity for people to earn college credit for what they have learned outside of a traditional classroom. Accepted or administered at more than 2,900 colleges and universities nationwide and approved by the American Council on Education (ACE), CLEP allows people to use their existing knowledge to fast-track their educational and professional goals.

WHY TAKE A CLEP EXAM?

CLEP is designed to address the fact that some individuals enrolling in college have already learned part of what is taught in college courses through job training, independent reading and study, noncredit adult courses, and advanced high school courses. CLEP provides these individuals a chance to show their mastery of college-level material by taking exams that assess their knowledge and skills.

CLEP is available to people in all stages:
- Adult learners
- College students
- Military service members
- Nontraditional students

Many adult learners pursuing college degrees face unique circumstances, including demanding work schedules, family responsibilities, tight budgets, and other constraints. Yet many adult learners also have years of valuable education and work experience that could be applied toward a degree. CLEP exams allow adult learners to capitalize on their prior learning and move forward with more advanced course work.

CLEP exams also benefit students who are currently enrolled in or are about to enroll in a college or university. With tuition costs on the rise, most students face financial challenges. The fee for a CLEP exam starts at $93 (plus any administrative fees of the testing facility)—significantly less than the average cost of a 3-hour college course. Students can maximize tuition savings by taking CLEP exams to earn college credit for introductory or mandatory course work. With a passing score on a CLEP exam, students are free to move on to higher-level course work in that subject, take desired electives, or focus on courses in a chosen major. Additionally, there are many nontraditional students who find that CLEP exams allow them to determine their own learning pace.

Including tuition and fees, the average cost of 1 college credit hour for students in 2022–2023 was
- $161 at two-year public in-district schools,
- $456 at four-year public in-state colleges,
- $1,177 at four-year public out-of-state colleges, and
- $1,642 at four-year private nonprofit colleges.

Source: Jennifer Ma and Matea Pender, *Trends in College Pricing and Student Aid 2022* (New York: College Board, 2022), https://research.collegeboard.org/media/pdf /trends-in -college-pricing-student-aid-2022.pdf.

Members of the armed services can initiate their post-military careers by taking CLEP exams in the areas they have experience. As an additional incentive, CLEP exams are funded for active military personnel through the Defense Activity for Non-Traditional Education Support (DANTES) program.

A variety of savings and benefits are available to help military service members, eligible spouses, and civil service employees reach their education goals:

- **Funded exam fees:** Eligible first-time test takers will have their exam fee funded by DANTES.
- **Waived administration fees:** Eligible test takers will have their administration fees waived at DANTES-funded test centers and all on-base military test centers.
- **Free examination guides:** Eligible test takers who register for a CLEP exam will receive a free CLEP exam guide through DANTES.

Finally, the CLEP program helps many students who might otherwise feel like college is out of reach because of the time, money, or effort required to earn the necessary credits for a degree. CLEP exams take two hours or less to complete. With good preparation, a test taker could earn credit for multiple college courses in a single weekend.

HOW DOES CLEP WORK?

CLEP offers 34 exams that cover material directly related to specific introductory-level college courses in the fields of history, social science, English composition, literature, natural science, mathematics, business, humanities, and world languages. Visit **https://clep.collegeboard.org/clep-exams** to explore the full catalog of exams.

Given the wide variety of subjects, it is important to know which colleges and universities offer credit for CLEP exams. It is likely that a college or university in your area offers credit, but you should confirm by contacting the school before you take an exam. Then review the list of CLEP exams to determine which ones are most relevant to the degree you are seeking and to your knowledge base.

Once you've confirmed that your school offers credit for CLEP exams, you can request that a copy of your score report be sent from College Board to the school you attend or plan to attend. The school will evaluate your score and determine whether to award you credit for or exempt you from the relevant course.

If the school awards you credit, the number of credits you have earned (ranging from 3 to 9, depending on the test subject) are recorded on your permanent record, indicating that you completed work equivalent to a course in that subject. If the school grants you an exemption to the course without credit, you'll be allowed to replace that course with one of your choice.

If you don't score enough points on the exam to earn credit from your school, take heart. You can retake the exam three months after the initial exam date. Even after paying the fee again, you'll still come out ahead in terms of time, money, and credit when you pass the exam.

CLEP TEST CENTERS

You can find a CLEP testing location at community colleges and universities across the country. Contact your local college or university to find out if the school administers CLEP exams, or visit **https://clep .collegeboard.org/find-a-test-center-and-schedule-your-test** to find a convenient location. Keep in mind that some colleges and universities administer CLEP exams only to enrolled students or waive administration fees for military service members whose exam fees are funded by DANTES. CLEP testing is also available to service members at military installations around the world.

CLEP Exams with Remote Proctoring

Test takers have the option to take CLEP exams at home with remote proctoring. Remote-proctored CLEP exams have the same timing, content, format, and on-screen experience as those administered at a test center. For registration and eligibility details, go to **https://clep.collegeboard.org/ about-remote-proctoring/take-clep-exam-remote-proctoring**.

HOW TO REGISTER FOR A CLEP EXAM

Follow these steps to register for a CLEP exam:

1. Sign in to My Account at **https://prod.idp.collegeboard.org** to choose your exam and the school(s) you want to receive your scores. (Test takers may send score reports to two institutions for free when they register. There is a $20 fee per score report for each additional institution.)
2. Pay for your exam(s).

3. Print your registration ticket.

4. Schedule your exam at your preferred test center. Write the test center address, contact information, and exam appointment details in the spaces provided on your ticket. Bring the ticket with you on test day.

Registering for a CLEP exam and scheduling it with a test center are separate steps.

Register, pay the fee, and print your ticket for the exam through the College Board website. Contact a test center directly to schedule the exam.

HOW TO PREPARE FOR A CLEP EXAM

Even if you are knowledgeable in a certain subject, you should still prepare for the exam to ensure that you achieve the highest score possible. The first step in studying for a CLEP exam is to find out what will be on the specific exam you have chosen. Information regarding exam content can be found in the individual CLEP exam's resource guide, accessed at **https://clep .collegeboard.org/clep-exams**. Each resource guide outlines the topics covered on the exam, as well as the approximate percentage of questions on each topic. Each resource guide also provides numerous sample questions just like those you'll see on test day, so you can get a basic sense of what to expect. Test questions are multiple choice with one correct answer choice and four incorrect answer choices.

In addition to the breakdown of assessed topics and sample questions, the resource guide also lists CLEP-recommended reference materials. If you do not own the recommended books, check college bookstores. Avoid paying high prices for new textbooks by looking online for used textbooks. Don't panic if you are unable to locate a specific textbook listed on the fact sheet; the textbooks are merely recommendations. Search for comparable books used in university courses on the subject. Current editions are ideal, and it is a good idea to use at least two different references when studying for a CLEP exam. The subject matter provided in this book will offer a sufficient review for most test takers, but if you determine that you need additional information as you read this book, it is a good idea to find a few other references.

The resource guide also includes information about the number of credit hours that ACE has recommended be awarded by colleges for a passing CLEP exam score. However, not all colleges and universities adhere to the ACE recommendations for CLEP credit hours. Some institutions require higher exam scores than the minimum scores recommended by ACE.

This book is your one-stop pocket guide to all the things you'll need to know for the exam. Each chapter provides an overview of one of the scoring categories, and **bold terms** throughout the book will identify the most important things you'll need to know. Use these terms to keep track of words and names that are likely to be on the exam and to guide any additional study you may need to do as you learn what the exam will include.

TEST DAY

Once you've reviewed the material and taken practice tests, you'll be ready to take your CLEP exam. Follow these tips for a successful test day experience.

1. **Arrive on time.** Not only is it courteous to arrive on time at the CLEP test center, but it also gives you plenty of time to take care of check-in procedures and settle into your surroundings.
2. **Bring proper identification.** CLEP testing facilities require that test takers bring a valid government-issued identification card with a current photo and signature. The first and last name on your ID must match the name on your registration ticket.
   - Acceptable forms of identification include a current driver's license, passport, military identification card, or state-issued identification card. Individuals who fail to bring proper identification will not be allowed to take the exam. For a detailed list of acceptable identification, visit **https://clep.collegeboard.org/test-day/what-to-bring-on-test-day**.
   - Military test takers should bring their Geneva Convention Identification Card. For more information on IDs for active-duty service members, spouses, and civil service civilian employees, visit **https://clep.collegeboard.org/clep-military-benefits**.
3. **Bring the items you will need.** Be sure to have the following items with you:
   - A valid registration ticket printed from the My Account registration portal

- Any required test center registration forms or printouts (Be sure to fill out all the necessary paperwork before test day!)
- Any additional administration fees (Each test center charges an additional fee and sets its own policy for payment.)

4. **Leave prohibited items at home.** These items are *not* allowed at the test center:
   - Electronic devices including smartphones, cell phones, mobile digital devices (e.g., iPads or tablets), cameras, headphones, smartwatches, and fitness bands
   - Reading material, textbooks, reference materials (including dictionaries and other study aids), scratch paper, and any other outside notes
   - Personal calculators (Calculators are integrated into the CLEP exam software where necessary.)

5. **Take the test.** During the exam, take the time to read each question and answer choice carefully. Eliminate the choices you know are incorrect to narrow down the number of potential answers. If a question completely stumps you, take an educated guess and move on to make the most of the 90 minutes you have for the exam.

INTRODUCTORY SOCIOLOGY EXAM OVERVIEW

The CLEP Introductory Sociology exam assesses your knowledge of the information covered in a standard one-semester introductory-level college sociology course. The exam does not assess your knowledge of advanced sociology concepts or methods. You will be required to demonstrate your basic knowledge and understanding of the subject and your ability to apply sociological theories and concepts.

According to the College Board (**https://clep.collegeboard.org/clep -exams/introductory-sociology**), you must be able to
- identify names, facts, and concepts from sociology;
- understand sociological methods and relationships between concepts, demographic trends, and theories of sociology;
- apply sociological concepts, theories, and methods to social situations; and
- analyze sociological data in charts and tables.

The 90-minute exam contains 100 questions, some of which are pretest questions that will not be scored. The exam divides questions into five categories within sociology. These are the categories and subcategories and their relative weights on the exam:

Institutions (20%)

- Family
- Education
- Economics
- Politics
- Religion
- Medicine

Social patterns (10%)

- Community
- Demography
- Human ecology and environmental sociology
- Rural and urban patterns

Social processes (25%)

- Social interaction
- Culture
- Socialization
- Deviance and social control
- Social change
- Collective behavior and social movements
- Groups and organizations

Social stratification (25%)

- Social class
- Social mobility
- Race and ethnic relations
- Sex and gender roles
- Aging
- Professions and occupations
- Power and social inequality

The sociological perspective (20%)

- History of sociology
- Sociological research methods
- Sociological theory

American Council on Education Credit Recommendations

Subject: Introductory Sociology
Credit Hours: 3
Minimum Score: 50

Source: American Council on Education. "College Board's College-Level Examination
Program," https://www.acenet.edu/National-Guide.
Note: Each institution may set its own credit-granting policy, which may differ from the
ACE recommendations.

Chapter 2

Study Strategies and Test-Taking Tips

OVERVIEW

- Study Strategies
- Mindset Strategies
- Test-Taking Tips

Having knowledge of the subject is paramount if you want to do well on a CLEP exam, but there are also ways to improve your chances of achieving a high score. This chapter will cover some study strategies, mindset strategies, and test-taking tips that can help with timed testing generally and with preparing for your CLEP Introductory Sociology exam using this book. Once you've reviewed the advice in this chapter, use the diagnostic test in Chapter 3 to evaluate your current skills and make a study plan.

STUDY STRATEGIES

There are myriad ways to approach studying for a CLEP exam. You've made a smart first step by purchasing this book or, perhaps, by signing up for more comprehensive study assistance at **www.petersons.com**. That said, learning the material is only part of the equation since you also need to be able to recall information in a high-pressure, timed testing environment. Being able to recall information when you need to is generally the result of effective studying and repetition. Use the following strategies to help you make the most of the significant effort you'll put into studying for your CLEP exam.

General Strategies

- **Don't wait until the last minute—start early!** Come up with a reasonable study plan and calendar early in your test-prep process and stick to it. Having a study plan allows you to make sure you understand the exam, evaluate what components you need to work on, and have plenty of time to review what you know and learn anything new.
- **Spread out your study sessions over time.** Most people are served better by several shorter study sessions spread out over time than they are by a lengthy cram session. It takes time to move things you learn into long-term memory, and the more time you give yourself to learn and review different concepts, the better you'll be able to recall them on test day. Because your brain needs time to process what it learns, spreading out your studying across multiple sessions is the best way to retain what you've learned.
- **Study regularly.** People need to return regularly to information they have learned to ensure that they remember it, so learners that complete periodic reviews of what they've learned are better able to retain the information. Studying regularly leading up to your exam is the best way to do this—it is far more effective than cramming, which offers few opportunities to practice recalling information, or studying sporadically, which leaves gaps during which you may forget what you've learned.
- **Study intensely rather than passively.** There is a documented relationship between stress and performance. Low-stress and high-stress situations both tend to negatively affect performance. However, there is a sweet spot: the right amount of pressure and intensity can improve performance, especially when learning. To study efficiently, you are best served by short, intense intervals. Languidly skimming over notes for hours on end will do significantly less than an hour of intentional active retrieval combined with paraphrasing, mind mapping new concepts, or answering timed practice questions.
- **Develop active learning practices.** Active learning involves planning, monitoring, and reflecting on your learning process. Here are some tips for active learning:
  - Plan out your work time.
  - Read carefully and strategically.
  - Take notes in some form.
  - Assess your progress regularly.
  - Spread out your study time.
  - Keep a regular schedule.

- ○ Create something while studying.
- ○ Use metacognitive techniques (such as reflective questions) to think about what you've learned so far and how you learned it.
- **Eliminate distractions.** Humans can multitask, but not very well—your divided attention is often the weakest of your attentive modes. To truly focus on the task of learning, you need to be able to isolate what you're trying to learn from other stimuli; this is how you ensure that what you learn can register properly. One of the most significant distractors for many (but not all) people is language, whether the lyrics of a song or the dialogue of a TV show playing in the background. If your brain struggles to filter out other voices, remove yourself from environments with lots of noise and leave your phone in another room so that you won't be distracted. Remember that you don't need to do this for long periods of time since your studying is more productive in intense bursts (an hour at a time) rather than in long, drawn-out cram sessions.
- **Encode new information meaningfully.** Memory always involves a process called encoding, wherein information moves from your senses to storage for later use. There are any number of tricks and tips for getting information to stick around, but one of the most effective ways is elaborative encoding. When you make information meaningful to you by connecting it to your own life and interests, it is easier for your brain to store that information for later use. For example, if you think about a real-life situation relevant to your own experiences that relates to the concept you are learning, you are more likely to remember it because you've encoded it in a way that holds meaning for you.
- **Divide tasks and information into chunks.** This technique can help anyone but is especially helpful for those who are having trouble focusing. Divide topics into smaller chunks of information rather than large blocks so you can deal with one chunk at a time. Resources (like this book) have organizational structures that may or may not suit your learning objectives. A chapter may cover a wide array of topics too extensive for your studying load on a given day or may not align with what you are trying to learn. In that situation, try to focus on one section, chart, or exercise at a time. Use different study strategies for different chunks of information so you don't feel overwhelmed. Reorganize resources in your notes and study materials based on relationships that you see, not necessarily what is prescribed by the resource itself. Consider what you can cover in the time you have for a given study session and focus only on that.

- **Vary topics and weave them together as you learn.** Alternate between topics while you study rather than dedicating large portions of time to a single topic. This applies to both what you review and self-quiz in your notes as well as to practice questions. While you're at it, look for connections between different topics. How does understanding one idea help you approach another? How do different concepts relate to each other? Reflecting on these connections as you study helps solidify concepts in your mind.
- **Create new materials as you study.** To retain and understand information, you need to both be able to recall it and be able to apply it. Exposure to information in different forms and in different ways helps your brain process it, but doing something with the information you're trying to learn really helps. Often, taking practice tests is one of the best ways to study, but mixing your methods before you get to the practice test can have positive results. You can try a variety of methods:
    - Create something using new information you acquire (e.g., write your own practice questions or tests).
    - Develop a visual aid that helps you make sense of new information.
    - Use different sensory modes—auditory, visual, or physical—to study.
    - Seek out additional resources to expand your research and understanding.
    - Create materials that help you engage in repetitive learning (e.g., make flash cards).
- **Regularly assess your retention and understanding.** Periodically check in with yourself and look for ways to test or elaborate on what you've learned so far. Find ways to assess your retention and understanding of new concepts using practice questions and tests or by trying to explain the concepts as if you were teaching them to someone else. Reflect on which categories and topics you have learned well and which may still need some improvement.
- **At the end of each study session, review and summarize what you learned.** This form of metacognition helps you make the most of your study time. By reflecting on what you learned and your thought processes and by summarizing new information, you are encoding that new information so you can recall it later. If you can't summarize a concept that you've just studied, devote more time to it in a future study session.

Strategies for Using This Book

In addition to the general study strategies, there are some specific ways you can use this book to help you prepare for your CLEP Introductory Sociology exam.

- **Use the Readiness Check and Test Yourself sections to help you assess your retention and understanding of new concepts.** Use these sections at the end of each content chapter to practice evaluating what you have learned and take note of what you need to review further.
- **Use the bold terms throughout this book to guide your study.** Each time you encounter a bold term in one of the content review chapters, use the opportunity to assess your knowledge. For each bold term you encounter, ask yourself the following questions:
  - Is this term completely new to me or have I heard it before?
  - If I've heard the term before, in what contexts have I heard it used?
  - Can I define the term in my own words based on what I know or have read?
  - What contextual information surrounds the term that can help me make sense of why it's important to the study of sociology?
  - Do I need to do further research to understand why this term is important?
  - Could there be a specific definition of this word that is important to sociologists?
- **Do additional outside research while you read this book.** This book attempts to cover the general information that any test taker needs to know for the CLEP Introductory Sociology exam, but no single book can be a complete substitute for a semester-long course. Use this book to help you figure out what you know and what you need to learn, then dive deeper if a topic seems unfamiliar. Visit your local library to find resources or talk to knowledgeable librarians who might be able to help you find information on topics that are new to you or that you don't fully understand.
- **Consider field-specific terminology when reviewing key terms and doing outside research.** In any field, there are terms that are specific to that field and used in contexts that would be immediately recognizable to scholars of that subject but not necessarily to outsiders. This is especially true in sociology: many familiar terms like *power*, *labor*, and *class* have specific contextual definitions that relate to the way sociologists talk about them. Don't just assume you know what a term

means because you've seen it before; instead, try and figure out how sociologists use it. Add search terms like *sociology* or *social sciences* to find field-specific uses of a term when searching online.

- **Use this book to guide your discussions with people who have taken an Introductory Sociology course.** If you know someone who has taken a course or the CLEP exam, ask them about the topics that are unfamiliar to you and ask them about topics they encountered most frequently. They will likely have insights that can help you and may even have materials you can borrow (such as class notes or old textbooks) as you study and do outside research.

MINDSET STRATEGIES

No matter which CLEP exam you take, maximizing the efficiency of your study time and approaching the test with the proper mindset can make a big difference in your performance.

Manage Your Time

While CLEP exams have rather forgiving time constraints compared with other standardized tests, time management is still a key issue and having the right mindset about it is important. A timed test does not have to cause anxiety or make you feel rushed—make a plan so you feel confident about how you will manage your time. For the CLEP Introductory Sociology exam, test takers have 90 minutes to complete 100 questions—this means that you should aim to answer each question in about 45 seconds or less. Many questions will be easy to answer and will take less time, leaving you more deliberation time for harder questions. Aim to eliminate the answers choices you can and make your best guess if you find yourself spending more than a minute or so on a question. Look for ways to save yourself time and move through the test efficiently without sacrificing accuracy.

Practice Testing Conditions

Test takers don't always think about the conditions under which they'll be testing on exam day, but the more you can mimic those conditions in practice, the more comfortable you'll be on test day. The diagnostic and practice tests in this book provide structure and time limits that can help re-create those conditions, but you may also want to consider your environment when you take the tests—try to mimic a testing environment and limit distractions that won't be present on the day you take the CLEP exam. By deliberately practicing testing under similar conditions, you will be practicing the mindset you want to have during the CLEP exam.

Evaluate the Stakes

You need to approach the CLEP exam with careful consideration of what is at stake for you. For example, if you must pass the exam to graduate or enter a program with prerequisites, the stakes are probably higher for you than for someone taking it on a whim to bypass an expensive elective course. Higher stakes do not mean you must have a higher level of anxiety —assessing what is at stake should help you determine the appropriate amount of time and effort to devote to preparation. Depending on your circumstances, you may be able to take the exam multiple times, but each attempt requires time and energy, so it is worth making the most of your opportunity. During the exam, you can remind yourself of how well you prepared for your goal.

Build Confidence

Your goal is to be as certain as possible about the correct answer when you answer a question. There are numerous strategies that can help you feel confident about your knowledge—many of which are in this book—but you need to know what they are and practice them. The good news is that as you become more adept at using these strategies, you will also become more confident in your ability to perform well on your exam. Confidence correlates positively with test performance, and building confidence is a valuable part of your test preparation.

TEST-TAKING TIPS

To maximize your performance on test day, there are several things to keep in mind in addition to your knowledge of the subject matter. Prioritizing these test-taking tips will help you manage important tasks on test day and perform your best on the exam.

Before Test Day

- **Understand the directions.** Luckily, the directions for the CLEP Introductory Sociology exam are straightforward—simply select the best of the five answer options for each multiple-choice question.

- **Know the expectations for each topic category.** Each of the content review chapters in this book (Chapters 4–8) covers one of the five testing categories of the CLEP Introductory Sociology exam, so reading this book will ensure that you understand what's expected of you. Revisit these chapters in the days leading up to your exam to remind yourself how questions for each topic differ, how many questions to expect from each category, and how to apply the strategies you developed during your study to approach different types of questions.
- **Make sure you are rested and ready.** No one wants to take an exam hungry or groggy. Plan far in advance to make the night before your exam a relaxing one: don't study that night (you'll be well prepared by then), have a filling and nutritious dinner, get to sleep early, wake in time for a similarly filling and nutritious breakfast, and then get to your testing site early so you can settle in and relax your mind before the exam begins.

On Test Day

- **Answer every question before time is called.** Follow your time management plan to ensure you answer every question. There is no penalty for guessing, so don't leave any questions unanswered. You can always note which answers you guessed and review them later. If you're running out of time, spend the last couple minutes of your exam guessing on all the questions that remain. Take time to eliminate answers you're pretty sure are incorrect first to improve your chance of guessing correctly—if you can eliminate two choices you know are incorrect, your chance of guessing correctly jumps from 1 in 5 to 1 in 3.
- **Use all the time you're allotted.** There is no such thing as "finishing early" with a timed test—use every minute you're given!
- **Make time for review.** Save time for review by following your time management plan. Use the time you have left to review your answers and return to more difficult questions, particularly those on which you had to guess.
- **Prioritize the questions you can answer with confidence.** As you take the exam, prioritize the easiest questions and those you feel most confident about first, then move on to harder questions. This way, you maximize the number of questions you are likely to get right. After you have answered all the questions, flip this priority arrangement— start by reviewing the questions you feel least confident about and then review those about which you feel more certain.

- **Be certain of your answers.** Don't just select an answer that seems right and call it a day. Review all the answer options and eliminate incorrect options as best you can so you can be more certain of the answer you do select even if you end up having to guess. Even when you feel confident about an answer, read the other options to make sure there isn't a better answer.
- **Guess as few answers as possible.** While it is better to guess than leave a question blank, your goal should still be to maximize the number of questions you can answer confidently. The more you practice time management and the more answer choices you can eliminate, the fewer answers you will have to guess.

These study strategies and test-taking tips will help you as you prepare for your CLEP exam. The more familiar you are with them and comfortable you are practicing them, the easier they will be to implement on test day. Return to this chapter as you read through the content chapters of this book and before you take the practice test in Chapter 9. By using these strategies and tips as you prepare, you'll be able to perform your best on your CLEP Introductory Sociology exam.

Chapter 3

Diagnostic Test

OVERVIEW

- Diagnostic Test
- Answer Key and Explanations
- Interpreting Your Diagnostic Test Results
- Evaluating Your Strengths and Areas for Improvement
- Setting Goals
- Creating a Study Plan
- Using This Book

An answer sheet for this test can be found on page 151.

DIAGNOSTIC TEST

This diagnostic test and the time allotted are a quarter of the length of a full CLEP Introductory Sociology exam.

25 Questions—23 Minutes

Directions: Each of the questions or incomplete statements below is followed by five suggested answers or completions. Select the one best answer for each. The Answer Key and Explanations will follow.

---

1. Which of the following had the most significant impact on the increase of suburbanization in the United States in the 1950s and 1960s?

   A. Increased number of women in the workforce
   B. Integration of public schools
   C. War protests
   D. Automation
   E. The Cold War

2. Mark did not complete high school and earned minimum wage for his work as a house cleaner. Eventually, he started his own company and hired employees, and now he earns an above-average salary. His career development is an example of

   A. meritocracy
   B. low status consistency
   C. high status consistency
   D. primogeniture
   E. class system

3. Marcia wants to study how references to technology in entertainment media have changed over the last decade. What type of research would be most appropriate for Marcia's analysis?

   A. Experimental research
   B. Field research
   C. Content analysis
   D. Secondary analysis
   E. Survey method

4. All of the following are examples of a hidden curriculum EXCEPT

A. practical skills like budgeting and civic participation

B. developing respect for authority figures like teachers and administrators

C. filling out a planner to keep track of important assignments

D. not speaking when another member of the class is speaking

E. using the bathroom between classes to avoid missing instruction

5. Which of the following types of authority does NOT have a set of rules for the transference of authority?

A. Traditional

B. Rational-legal

C. Charismatic

D. Representative democracy

E. Monarchy

6. A sociologist who studies human ecology is interested in which of the following?

A. The study of genetics and heredity in human populations

B. The exploration of ancient civilizations and their cultural practices

C. The analysis of how human activities impact and are impacted by the environment(s) in which they take place

D. The examination of economic systems and their impact on global trade

E. The study of how individuals create and interpret symbols in daily interactions with others

7. A city cannot develop without

A. a population of young adults who are ready to move to a new area

B. an agricultural surplus

C. two or more developing industries

D. enough available housing to accommodate a minimum annual population increase of 4%

E. a public transportation system

8. Which of the following is an example of an aggregate?

   A. Baby boomers

   B. A book club

   C. Members of a professional sports team

   D. People in a grocery store

   E. A teachers union

9. Tiana is an American student studying abroad in Italy. She is surprised and frustrated to find that she cannot grocery shop on Sundays because the stores are closed. This is an example of

   A. cultural relativism

   B. cultural imperialism

   C. culture shock

   D. xenocentrism

   E. ideal culture

10. Which of the following is an example of violating a more?

   A. Failing to hold the door open for the person behind you

   B. Cutting to the front of a long line

   C. Fleeing the scene of a car crash

   D. Refusing to shake someone's hand when meeting them

   E. Wearing jeans to a black-tie wedding

11. All of the following characteristics are commonly attributed to pink-collar jobs EXCEPT

   A. a historical association with the service sector

   B. low relative pay

   C. a historical association with women

   D. limited growth potential

   E. strict education requirements

12. Chelsea is a first-generation college graduate who became CEO of a technology company. Her parents worked in customer service. This is an example of

   A. intergenerational mobility

   B. downward mobility

   C. intragenerational mobility

   D. primogeniture

   E. high status consistency

13. Which of the following terms is used to describe a small community characterized by strong social bonds and shared values?

   A. Anomie
   B. *Verstehen*
   C. *Gemeinschaft*
   D. *Gesellschaft*
   E. Alienation

14. In sociological terminology, a study of the behavioral differences between new and regular customers conducted by a sociologist working as a waiter at a restaurant would be called which of the following?

   A. Survey research
   B. Case study
   C. Laboratory experiment
   D. Small group experiment
   E. Participant observation

15. Émile Durkheim defined religion as having three elements, including

   A. beliefs, texts, and buildings
   B. beliefs, practices, and community
   C. practices, leaders, and community
   D. texts, leaders, and values
   E. community, influence, and texts

16. Which of the following is a latent function of primary and secondary education?

   A. Bullying
   B. Childcare
   C. Literacy
   D. Socialization
   E. Understanding of civic values

17. Sociological studies of the medical field in the United States show that

   A. physicians take women's and men's health complaints equally seriously
   B. physicians take men's health complaints less seriously than women's health complaints
   C. childbirth is significantly more dangerous for Black women than it is for white women
   D. childbirth is significantly more dangerous for Asian women than it is for Black women
   E. physicians are more likely to provide preventive care to a patient of their own race

18. Which of the following theoretical perspectives would be most useful in understanding the value that social programs like public education, access to health care, and high civic participation can add to society as a whole?

   A. Conflict theory
   B. Symbolic interactionism
   C. Structural functionalism
   D. Feminist theory
   E. Postmodernism

19. Which of the following theoretical perspectives would support the idea that social stratification only benefits some members of society?

   A. Functionalism
   B. Symbolic interactionism
   C. Conspicuous consumption
   D. Conflict theory
   E. Status consistency

20. When people participate in activities that break cultural norms but do so in a place or at a time that is designated for that purpose in order to provide temporary relief from the societal pressure to meet norms, it is known as

    A. a moral holiday
    B. a positive sanction
    C. a negative sanction
    D. a moral break
    E. counterculture

21. Which of the following statements is true of deviance?

    A. Deviance is always considered a crime.
    B. Deviance is standard across cultures.
    C. Deviance is determined not by the act itself but by the reaction to the act.
    D. Deviant acts are only committed by those in the counterculture.
    E. There is a small minority of the population that displays deviant behavior.

22. Which term refers to the phenomenon in which individuals from underrepresented groups are brought into organizations to give the appearance of diversity without significantly changing its existing power structures?

    A. Tokenism
    B. Affirmative action
    C. Equal opportunity
    D. Reverse discrimination
    E. Assimilation

23. Which research method involves an in-depth, long-term study of a single individual, group, or community, often using a variety of data sources?

    A. Survey research
    B. Experimental research
    C. Content analysis
    D. Case study
    E. Participant observation

24. Passing a bar exam, working one's way up the corporate ladder to a leadership position, and graduating from a prestigious university are all examples of

A. role sets
B. cultural roles
C. achieved statuses
D. ascribed statuses
E. mobility aspirations

25. Which of the following statements is the most accurate description of the concept of the looking-glass self?

A. A person's concept of self is developed and influenced by the reactions of others.
B. A person's physical body influences the reactions of others.
C. A person's physical body influences their self-perception.
D. Self-reflection influences socialization.
E. A person's concept of self is developed and influenced by images from the media.

ANSWER KEY AND EXPLANATIONS

1. B	6. C	11. E	16. B	21. C
2. B	7. B	12. A	17. C	22. A
3. C	8. D	13. C	18. C	23. D
4. A	9. C	14. E	19. D	24. C
5. C	10. C	15. B	20. A	25. A

1. **The correct answer is B.** The integration of public schools increased suburbanization as white families left the cities for the suburbs to avoid sending their children to integrated schools, a process known as "white flight."

2. **The correct answer is B.** Status consistency measures the flexibility of a person's social status or rank within a society. More flexible societies have lower status consistency and more rigid societies have higher status consistency. This is an example of low status consistency because Mark's socioeconomic status was flexible and changed over time despite his lower education level.

3. **The correct answer is C.** Content analysis would be the most productive research method for Marcia because it would allow her to analyze existing entertainment media and draw generalizations from her findings. Since her goal is to track changes in the media itself, rather than audience reactions or viewership data, the other choices would not offer useful information.

4. **The correct answer is A.** The hidden curriculum refers to the skills and lessons informally and indirectly taught to students through the education system, such as obedience and conformity, rather than specific content aligned with academic standards, such as the skills described in choice A.

5. **The correct answer is C.** Charismatic authority does not have a set structure for the transfer of authority in the way that the other answer options have protocols for the transfer of authority. Max Weber, who developed the concept, identified several possible methods of succession, but since the authority under this system is concentrated in the leader, the death or abdication of that leader constitutes the end of their authority.

6. **The correct answer is C.** Human ecology is the exploration of the impact of people on their environment and the environment's impact on people. While the other choices could be a part of the larger study, choice C best summarizes the main goal of sociologists who study human ecology.

7. **The correct answer is B.** A city cannot develop without an agricultural surplus that can sustain a growing population and support other economic activities that exist outside of the urban center. While the other choices certainly exist in some, or even most, cities, choice B is the only answer that is essential in all cases.

8. **The correct answer is D.** An aggregate is a group of people who are in the same place at the same time but do not share a sense of identity and do not interact, such as people in a grocery store. Each of the other choices are examples of groups with either a shared identity (choices A and D) or that require interaction (choices B and E).

9. **The correct answer is C.** Tiana experiences culture shock at the differences between the two countries. While it may be common to grocery shop on Sundays in the United States, grocery stores in Italy have different norms surrounding that practice, which is the source of her frustration.

10. **The correct answer is C.** Mores are defined as strict determiners between right and wrong, and deviations from them are often punished. They are contrasted with folkways, which are less serious determinations of right and wrong that are only enforced through social pressure. Fleeing the scene of a car crash is a crime that can have serious consequences and is nearly universally considered to be wrong, making it a more. The other answer choices are violations of folkways.

11. **The correct answer is E.** Pink-collar jobs are positions within the workforce that have traditionally been filled by women. They are often within the service sector, offer lower pay compared with blue- and white-collar jobs, and, historically, have not offered significant potential for growth in pay or prestige (a phenomenon known as "the glass ceiling"). While access to higher education has grown for women in the latter half of the 20th century and early decades of the 21st century, pink-collar jobs are not associated with strict education requirements as women have not had equitable access to colleges and universities.

12. **The correct answer is A.** Intergenerational mobility is any change in social class between generations of a family. Choice B is incorrect because Chelsea achieves higher social status than her parents, moving upward and not downward. Choice C, intragenerational mobility, refers to differences in social class between members of the same generation. Choice D is incorrect because primogeniture is the right of succession of a first-born child, which is unrelated, and choice E is incorrect because high status consistency would indicate a society in which the kind of mobility Chelsea experienced would be uncommon or impossible.

13. **The correct answer is C.** *Gemeinschaft*, conceptualized by Ferdinand Tönnies and developed further by Max Weber, refers to a close-knit community that shares values and strong bonds with each other.

14. **The correct answer is E.** Participant observation is when a researcher assumes a role in a specific context to observe behavior within that context, such as the situation described in this question. This is also an example of ethnographic research since the sociologist is participating in the social environment they are observing.

15. **The correct answer is B.** Durkheim defined religion as a set of beliefs and practices that unite a group of people into a moral community.

16. **The correct answer is B.** Childcare is a latent function of the education system, meaning it is a function that is persistent but not stated. Choice A (bullying) is a dysfunction. Choices C, D, and E are manifest functions of education, meaning they are persistent and stated.

17. **The correct answer is C.** In the United States, Black women experience a disproportionately higher risk of maternal mortality because of internalized societal biases, scientific blind spots, and statistically lower socioeconomic status and access to health care. The other choices are not supported by data trends related to this subject.

18. **The correct answer is C.** Structural functionalism is a theoretical framework that posits that each social institution is integral to the continued success of a society and provides benefits to society as a whole. This question presents common social institutions that provide broad benefits to society beyond the individuals who utilize their services, so choice C is the correct answer.

19. **The correct answer is D.** Conflict theory states that society competes for access to resources. Those in power hold the majority of the resources, which, in turn, causes scarcity of resources for the oppressed. Functionalism (choice A) emphasizes the interdependencies inherent in society, which does not match the question, and the other choices represent smaller sociological processes rather than a larger theoretical perspective.

20. **The correct answer is A.** A moral holiday is a socially designated time or place in which people are allowed to break some cultural norms without incurring the consequences they typically would. Examples from the United States might include celebrating Mardi Gras, attending certain music festivals, or going on a trip to a party destination like Las Vegas. Though moral holidays may be governed by different values and norms than the broader culture, they are not considered countercultural because they exist only in a specific place and/or time.

21. The correct answer is C. According to Howard S. Becker, deviance is not an inherent quality of an act but rather a label assigned to an act based on society's reaction to it. Deviant behavior varies across cultures, and whether an act is considered deviant depends on how society perceives it.

22. The correct answer is A. Tokenism is the practice of including individuals from underrepresented groups in organizations to help the organization appear diverse while it maintains its existing power structures. Affirmative action (choice B) and equal opportunity laws (choice C) both explicitly seek to change existing power structures. Reverse discrimination (choice D) does not fit the question as it impacts the dominant group within a society. Assimilation (choice E) generally occurs at the state or national level, rather than the organizational level, which makes it less applicable to the given situation than choice A.

23. The correct answer is D. A case study is a research method that entails conducting long-term and detailed examination of a single group or individual.

24. The correct answer is C. Education level, economic success achieved through hard work, and membership in a respected profession are all examples of status obtained by achievement. Roles (choices A and B) are socially defined rights, duties, and expectations that people are expected to fill. Since none of these examples are specifically expected of a group of people, this eliminates both choices. Ascribed statuses (choice D) are assigned to people, rather than earned. The term *mobility aspirations* (choice E) refers to the embedded idea that people should move up in the social order, which relates to the criteria of the question but cannot be confirmed without further context.

25. The correct answer is A. Charles Horton Cooley created the concept of the looking-glass self, which refers to the way a person's self-concept is influenced and developed by their perception of the reactions of the people around them. Each of the other options may be true, and they are even related to parts of the larger theory, but choice A is the best summary of the concept as a whole.

INTERPRETING YOUR DIAGNOSTIC TEST RESULTS

Now that you've taken the diagnostic test to establish a baseline, it's time to interpret your score. The purpose of a diagnostic test is exactly what it sounds like—it diagnoses your strengths and weaknesses so you can make informed decisions about how you want to study going forward. While this diagnostic test is only a quarter of the length of the full 100-question CLEP Introductory Sociology exam, the ratio of question types and the time allotted reflect the conditions of the full-length exam. CLEP uses a formula to convert your raw score into a scaled score ranging from 20 to 80, so your raw score doesn't translate exactly into your final score on the exam, but your performance on this diagnostic test can help you determine the areas where you might want to direct your focus when studying.

The CLEP Introductory Sociology exam covers five distinct testing categories, each of which are weighted differently.

Category	Percentage of Total Questions
Institutions	20%
Social patterns	10%
Social processes	25%
Social stratification	25%
The sociological perspective	20%

Let's look at your diagnostic test scores by category. Record your score for each category in the following chart.

MY DIAGNOSTIC TEST SCORES BY CATEGORY		
Category	**Question Numbers**	**Raw Score**
Institutions	4, 5, 15, 16, 17	_____ /5
Social patterns	1, 6, 7	_____ /3
Social processes	8, 9, 10, 18, 20, 21	_____ /6
Social stratification	2, 11, 12, 19, 22, 24	_____ /6
The sociological perspective	3, 13, 14, 23, 25	_____ /5
Total Raw Score		_____ /25
Full Test Raw Score Projection*		_____ /100

* Multiply total raw score by 4

EVALUATING YOUR STRENGTHS AND AREAS FOR IMPROVEMENT

Now that you can see how you performed in each category, reflect on your strengths and areas for improvement.

- What went well for you during the diagnostic test? Which categories were easiest for you?
- What did you struggle with during the diagnostic test? Which categories were hardest for you?
- After your experience, what are some things you want to keep in mind as you study?

Let's look at an example of a hypothetical test taker's diagnostic test scores and self-evaluation as a guide to help you pinpoint your strengths and areas for improvement in the context of the scoring categories.

DIAGNOSTIC TEST SELF-EVALUATION EXAMPLE			
Full Test Raw Score Goal: 70/100			
Category	**Correct Answers**	**Strengths**	**Areas for Improvement**
Institutions	4/5	I had a good working knowledge of major institutions and methods.	I need a better understanding of different theorists' ideas about social institutions.
Social patterns	0/3	I recognized some important vocabulary terms.	I need to recognize more of the theorists' names.
Social processes	1/6	It did not take me a long time to answer these questions.	I need to understand the difference between key terms.
Social stratification	5/6	I knew most of the terms and methods mentioned.	I need to manage my time better because these questions took me longer to answer than others.
The sociological perspective	3/5	I understand methods well.	I could learn more about the early history of sociology.
Raw Score	**13/25**	I understand sociological methods and institutions pretty well.	In general, I need to pay more attention to theorists, important terms, and the history of sociology.
Full Test Raw Score Projection*	**52/100**		

* Multiply raw score by 4

Now fill in your answers based on your diagnostic test results. Try to evaluate your strengths and areas for improvement in each category.

DIAGNOSTIC TEST SELF-EVALUATION			
Full Test Raw Score Goal: _____ /100			
Category	Correct Answers	Strengths	Areas for Improvement
Institutions	_____ /5		
Social patterns	_____ /3		
Social processes	_____ /6		
Social stratification	_____ /6		
The sociological perspective	_____ /5		
Raw Score	_____ /25		
Full Test Raw Score Projection*	_____ /100		

* Multiply raw score by 4

Keep these reflections in mind as you set goals for yourself and create a study plan.

SETTING GOALS

Now that you've reflected on your diagnostic test experience, think about your goals. If you decided to take your exam tomorrow without any further preparation, and you did things the exact same way, you would likely perform the same way you did on the diagnostic test. Since you are using this book, you likely have some time to prepare for the exam, which means you have ample opportunity to improve your performance.

As a CLEP test taker, your general goal is to maximize the number of questions you answer correctly so that you have the best chance of scoring high enough to earn credit. The American Council of Education (ACE) recommends a scaled score of 50 (on a scale of 20 to 80) as a credit-earning score for CLEP Introductory Sociology and most other CLEP exams. However, individual schools may require a higher score than ACE recommends. Be sure to verify that your institution(s) of choice accept(s) CLEP Introductory Sociology exams for credit, then find out the minimum credit-earning scaled score required. Please note that the process for calculating a scaled score from a raw score varies by test subject and test form. There is no universal way to determine whether your raw score will earn you credit. However, the common guidance is that answering 70% of questions correctly (70/100 for the CLEP Introductory Sociology exam) will put you near the ACE-recommended score. That value can act as a general goal, but first prioritize building on your strengths and addressing the areas of improvement that you identified in your Diagnostic Test Self-Evaluation. From there, you can set a score goal that works for you and make a study plan to achieve it.

CREATING A STUDY PLAN

When creating a study plan, your first order of business should be to determine how much time you have to devote to preparation. If you have an hour a day for several months, you'll probably approach things differently than someone who is trying to study as comprehensively in two weeks. Figure out how much time you have and set a reasonable goal for how much studying you would like to do in that time. Then, divide up the amount of preparation time you have according to your study priorities. Only you can determine the best way to do this. However, your diagnostic test offers helpful clues about how to do this most effectively.

Determining What to Study

The hypothetical test taker achieved a raw score of 13/25 on their diagnostic test, which would translate to a raw score of 52 on a full-length exam. They are aiming for a raw score of 70, meaning they'll need to improve by 18 points to achieve their goal. The test taker can now use this information to plan their study time.

The test taker should start by looking at the categories in which they performed best: institutions and social stratification. It might seem like this test taker doesn't need to spend any time studying for these categories; however, those high scores mean that these are their strongest categories, so it might be an easy place for them to pick up extra points to make up for the categories that are harder for them. The test taker should consider areas for improvement in these subject areas—they noted that managing time and becoming more familiar with theorists would help most—and then make sure to address those weak spots. They may not spend as much time studying for these categories as the others, but they should devote some study time to their best categories to improve their score.

Next, the test taker should consider the category in which they had the lowest performance: in this case, social patterns. Luckily for this test taker, that category has a lower weight relative to the others. However, the 10 questions that will be in this category on the exam are still important to the test taker's overall score. Even with the lower category weight, the test taker has the most room to improve in this category and should plan to spend a bit of extra time studying for it. Their reflections note that one area for improvement was recognizing the names of important theorists, so when they are studying social patterns (Chapter 5 in this book), they will want to pay extra attention to the names of theorists. They should also look into any recommended tips and strategies for tackling difficult questions and categories (Chapter 2 in this book).

The test taker should continue to apply this analytical process to the remaining categories and consider how much room there is for improvement and how they can use the strategies that will help them most. For example, the test taker noted that in multiple categories, they excelled at questions related to sociological methods. Consequently, their studying should focus more on other areas. That doesn't mean that they should neglect sociological research methods entirely, only that other skills should be prioritized.

Creating a Study Schedule

After the test taker has analyzed their diagnostic test results and prioritized their study plan by category, they can create a schedule. Let's say our
test taker has 1 hour per weekday for 5 weeks to study for their exam. At
the end of the 5 weeks, they plan to take a practice test (Chapter 9 in this
book) a week before their official exam, saving time for any last-minute
review based on the results of their practice test. This test taker has 25 total
hours to devote to studying before their practice test and 5 more available
for review after the practice test. Accordingly, they might plan their time
as follows:

Social patterns	7 Hours
Social processes	7 Hours
The sociological perspective	5 Hours
Social stratification	3 Hours
Institutions	2 Hours
Review before practice test	1 Hour
Review after practice test	5 Hours

It's a good idea to approach this plan flexibly and adjust as you progress. If
the test taker felt confident they had reviewed social patterns thoroughly
after 6 hours of study and decided to spend a spare hour on another category instead, that would still be a perfectly suitable plan. The test taker
could even break down their study plan by day to stay on track.

STUDY PLAN EXAMPLE					
	Monday	Tuesday	Wednesday	Thursday	Friday
Week 1	Social patterns	Social processes	The sociological perspective	Social processes	Social stratification
Week 2	Social patterns	Social processes	Social patterns	The sociological perspective	Institutions
Week 3	Social patterns	Social processes	Social patterns	The sociological perspective	Institutions
Week 4	Social patterns	Social processes	The sociological perspective	Social processes	Social stratification
Week 5	Social patterns	Social processes	The sociological perspective	Social stratification	Review
Week 6	Review concepts missed on the practice test				

Of course, you can allot your study hours in any way that makes sense for you—and not everyone will be able to plan their studying in such an orderly fashion. Some test takers will also benefit from focusing on more than one category in each study session. Nonetheless, creating a specific study calendar that dedicates time to different categories and for returning to them later for review is a good idea. It also is a good reminder that multiple repetitions correlate with a better chance of meeting your score goals. Plan to include variety and ample opportunity to review categories you have already studied. If you follow this study plan example, by the time you take your practice test, you will be thoroughly prepared to improve your score.

USING THIS BOOK

Remember that a CLEP exam isn't just about what you know but also how well you can remember foundational details across the entirety of the material covered in a semester-long course. The diagnostic test provides a snapshot of how you might perform on your CLEP exam, but it's not the entire picture—you also likely know which aspects of the subject matter you know better, and which will require more review. Use your diagnostic test to form an initial study plan but recognize that you may need to adjust how you divide your study time as you review the five categories covered on the exam. Each category is covered in Chapters 4–8.

As a reminder, the **bold key terms** throughout this book highlight important concepts that are likely to come up on your exam. Alongside the study plan you make based on your diagnostic test results, these bold key terms can help guide any research you may need to do beyond this guide to feel fully prepared for your CLEP exam. As with all CLEP exams, you may still encounter questions about more obscure topics than those presented in this guide, so utilize any other sociology knowledge or resources you have as you work through the content categories. You can also find a wealth of supplementary materials to fill out your study plan—including full-length practice tests, videos, and interactive presentations—at **www.petersons .com/testprep/clep/**.

Chapter 4

Institutions

OVERVIEW
- Family
- Education
- Economics
- Politics
- Religion
- Medicine
- Conclusion
- Readiness Check: Institutions
- Test Yourself: Institutions

The study of social institutions is a major field of sociology, and 20% of the questions on the CLEP Introductory Sociology exam address this topic. Institutions are social constructions that organize various aspects of people's social lives. They can be formal organizations, informal groups, sets of rules, or social norms, but at their core, they work to shape and regulate individual behavior.

Social institutions provide the foundation for social structure—they help people understand the rules, norms, and expectations of their society. All aspects of everyday life are governed by social institutions, from large-scale institutions like national governments and economic systems that influence millions to small-scale institutions like families that teach the basics of being human. Often, institutions work to preserve social stability by encouraging people to act in ways that fit into and support the status quo.

Sociologists have identified many social institutions, but some of the most important are those that govern behavior in the following categories.
- Family
- Education

- Economics
- Politics
- Religion
- Medicine

Sociologists are interested in understanding how institutions in each of these categories affect human behavior, how they shape opinions and opportunities through the rules and norms they endorse, and how they encourage people to act in certain ways. Of course, social institutions are human-made phenomena, so sociologists also study how they come into being and how they transform and change over time. In this chapter, we will explore each of the six primary institutions in social life and assess their impact on everyday life and social structures.

FAMILY

The family is one of the most important social institutions because it is one of the first to affect and shape individuals as members of society. Sociologists refer to families as the **primary agent** of socialization. **Socialization** is the process by which people learn what is expected of them as members of society and internalize the unspoken rules and norms that structure and guide social life.

For most people, families provide the foundation of the socialization process. They teach the basic building blocks for becoming functional members of society. Families are particularly powerful in this regard for several reasons. Families are most people's first introduction to the world; most people encounter and are shaped by their families before they are old enough to interact with almost anyone else. Throughout childhood, most people are immersed in family life, spending a great deal of time with their family members. Families also generally have a vested interest in shaping individuals into the people they will become; many families consider it their responsibility to raise children and teach them the social skills necessary to become part of the world around them.

Families teach the practical skills of social life, such as feeding, bathing, and clothing. They also teach the more complex skills of managing social relationships and relationships with the outside world. All family teaching includes teaching about **values**. Values are important perspectives on the world that shape beliefs and help people make sense of the world. Values help form morals and shape interactions with others. Attitudes toward other institutions—such as religious, political, or economic institutions—are generally learned from family. These perspectives on life help shape the way people experience and relate to the world.

But what *is* a family? What groups and relationships can be considered families, and how has this institution changed over time? In the United States, primacy has historically been placed on the concept of the **nuclear family**, an idealized version of a distinct family unit that consists of two heterosexual parents and their children. In reality, families are often much more complicated than the nuclear model. Family units of all shapes and sizes, both biological and found, can fulfill the institutional role of the family. Moreover, there is evidence that the norms about what constitutes a family have been evolving significantly in the United States in recent decades. More children than ever grow up in **single-parent households**, and divorce has become increasingly common. The legalization and growing acceptance of **same-sex marriage** has also redefined what many Americans consider to be a family unit.

Evidence shows that the circumstances of birth and family affect what sociologist **Max Weber** described as **life chances**. Weber defined life chances as the types of opportunities and options a person has as they grow up. Think, for example, of the differences that might exist between the opportunities available to the child of a wealthy couple in Manhattan or Beverly Hills and those available to a child from a poor family in rural Appalachia or a single-parent household in an impoverished inner-city neighborhood. Families, then, are an important component of a society's **social stratification**—the categorization used to differentiate people in society—which we will discuss in depth in Chapter 7.

In this way and many others, institutions like the family are intimately connected with institutions in other areas of social life. Though families provide powerful learning experiences and set the conditions for their family members' early social world, they always do so as part of a larger network of social realities and power structures. This network, in turn, is shaped by all the social institutions that govern collective behavior. Institutions never exist in a vacuum, no matter how primary a particular institution (like family) may seem to a person's social development.

EDUCATION

The education system is another powerful institution, and it is one of the most important institutions for determining whether the influence of the family is muted or strengthened. Sociologists see education as a **secondary agent** of socialization; people start school after they have mastered many of the types of skills instilled by family life, and the skills taught in educational institutions build on those basics.

Most people first learn to interact with others outside the family unit and close family friends through the education system. The start of school also typically correlates with an increased awareness of **diversity** as people become aware that there are others in society with ideas, values, behaviors, and experiences that differ from their own. At school, students begin to learn a second set of values that, in contrast to the internal focus of family life, is focused externally. As they learn about their place in the world, school-aged people begin to expand the scope of their perspectives.

One of the primary functions of education as an institution is to re-create the social conditions that make people productive members of society. Schools teach practical skills that are necessary to succeed in adult life and the working world, such as reading, writing, and mathematical skills. Educational institutions also condition people to follow a daily schedule and strive to instill a work ethic and love of learning, skills perceived to be beneficial to personal development. Schools are also responsible for teaching **civic** and social virtues. It is no accident that school children throughout the United States are often required to say the Pledge of Allegiance each morning or are taught national and state histories and the value of social engagement and volunteerism.

Topics that are outside of the academic curriculum but essential to social life and thereby still taught in school are sometimes called a **hidden curriculum**. A hidden curriculum can include nonacademic teaching, such as socioemotional learning, but it can also include unwritten rules and expectations that students are expected to internalize. Students who enter the education system without an understanding of the underlying logic and standard practices of the institution sometimes may struggle to understand these unspoken social expectations.

The power of education systems in shaping people's relationships to society means that they, too, have a significant influence on life chances. Sociologists have long asserted that education is the single most powerful means of changing a person's life circumstances. Yet, like the family, educational institutions are sensitive to interactions with institutions in other social realms. In the United States, **public schools** are often funded by property taxes levied from the surrounding areas. This funding model means that schools in wealthier areas, where **property taxes** are likely to be high, tend to be better funded than schools in poorer areas. Consequently, it is difficult to talk about public education in an institutional sense without discussing how economic and political institutions affect education. School funding matters—better funded schools can afford to provide more **extracurricular opportunities**, hire better teachers, and offer advanced courses that better prepare students for success in the workplace. **Private and charter schools**, too, often offer different opportunities to those whose families can afford tuition. **School voucher** programs that allow parents to redirect federal money to support their children's enrollment in private schools have been controversial. Those in favor of such policies argue that they support a wider range of choices and specialized options to suit the needs of students and their families. Those who oppose school voucher programs argue that their benefits are outweighed by their contribution to the continued defunding of public education, and some question the constitutionality of federal funding for charter schools, many of which are religiously affiliated educational institutions. School voucher programs are thus a great example of the intersection between educational, political, economic, and religious institutions.

Education systems also impact adult students at the **higher education** level. The American higher education system encompasses a wide range of institutions, including four-year colleges and universities, two-year community colleges, and trade and vocational schools. Just as with K–12 education, many debates have been waged over state and federal funding for institutions of higher education.

Controversies around higher education extend beyond funding levels, however, to the purpose of higher education. Some think that higher education should be chiefly focused on **marketable skills**, teaching subjects and offering majors that directly correlate with the needs of the employment market. Some argue that limiting the focus of higher education to what the economy deems marketable is problematic. Market values shift frequently, and workers trained to meet the needs of one moment may not find opportunities in the next. Others argue that higher education should actually have a heavier emphasis on **liberal arts**, including skills and systems of thought that transcend job skills and create well-rounded,

civic-minded individuals capable of critical thought and social engagement. Here, too, debates have raged about the politics of education: Are
programs exploring issues such as gender or race and ethnicity valuable
efforts toward **social justice**? Or are they overtly political attempts to
change society's views on such subjects and designate which fields of study
are considered valuable in the contemporary era.

ECONOMICS

Economic institutions have a powerful effect on public and private life.
Economic systems determine a person's capacity to secure the necessities
of everyday life, such as food, clothing, and housing. The economy is also
one of the most important institutions when it comes to a person's life
chances. In fact, since the field of sociology began, most sociologists have
argued that economic institutions are one of the foundational elements of
social structure, shaping and structuring human life.

Some **materialist** scholars, such as **Karl Marx**, believed that a society's
mode of production—how it produces the goods and services necessary
for the business of living—powerfully influences the shape that society
will take. In his efforts to understand the origins of capitalism, Marx
researched what he considered to be an evolution of the modes of production. He outlined how **primitive tribal societies** evolved into societies
based on **slave labor**, then **feudalism**, and then **capitalism** before elaborat-
ing his own theories on **socialism** and **communism**. Marx and others saw
these shifts in production as revolutionizing society's **division of labor**,
effecting the way decisions were made about how jobs and responsibilities ought to be divided among members of a society. French sociologist
Émile Durkheim argued that this transition moved society from a state of
mechanical solidarity, wherein homogeneity encouraged social cohesion,
to one of **organic solidarity**, wherein people and institutions each fulfilled
different roles in social life, much like different organs do in an organism.

Changes like these required a simultaneous reconfiguration of social life.
In the transition from feudalism to capitalism, for example, Marx identified a shift in **labor** production from artisanal craftsmanship to industrialized **mass production**. This transition encouraged laborers to leave
rural farms in pursuit of what they thought would be better and higher
paying jobs. The subsequent mass migration to big cities led to a new age
of **urbanism**, when, for the first time in history, more people lived in cities
than rural environments. It also changed the ways people related to each

other. Marx and those who followed him were very critical of many of the conditions that underlaid this transition. They argued that the shift to industrialized mass production had robbed humans of their humanity, alienating them from each other, the products of their labor, and even what it meant to be human.

Sociologists have also examined other ways in which economic institutions impact human life. Scholars of **globalization** argue that economic institutions and the search to maximize profits have encouraged the integration of the world into one massive economic system. Under the **world economic system**, countries and international companies trade with each other and compete to obtain greater economic advantages. This system enables the rapid transfer of goods, services, and even cultures and ideologies around the world, a process that has increasingly sped up as new technologies have made communication, trade, and travel even easier. A student in Illinois might be wearing blue jeans made in China while ordering coffee at a shop featuring blends from Brazil and Kenya. They might drive a German car to dinner at an Italian restaurant where their food was prepared by an immigrant from Mexico and use a cell phone that relies on technology from Japan. This type of **fluidity** and exchange has had profound effects on every world culture and our collective, global understanding of the world.

Within their own country or society, a person's work and livelihood depend on a complicated infrastructure of economic production and exchange. Economists often differentiate **sectors of the economy** by their type of production.

SECTORS OF THE ECONOMY

Economic Sector	Production Classification
Primary	Raw materials
Secondary	Manufacturing
Tertiary	Services
Quaternary	Knowledge

Together, the **primary**, **secondary**, **tertiary**, and **quaternary** sectors make up a society's economy, and their relative balance within that society helps determine the type of economy and the type of opportunities available to members of that society. The configuration of these economic sectors determines how people get the goods they need to survive, how they make enough money to support themselves, and even what they enjoy and how they perceive culture. It is no exaggeration, then, to assert that economic institutions shape much of a person's experience of the world.

POLITICS

Many economic structures and institutions are influenced by and intimately related to political institutions. **Societies** are collections of people who live together in an **organized community**. When that community has **self-determination**, meaning members of a society have control over the society's functioning, it is called a **state** (another term for a country or nation). States are powerful organizations that play an important role in human life. On a macro scale, states are responsible for protecting their people, fielding armies, and securing **borders** in a way that, theoretically, supports the interests of their own people over the interests of people from other states.

In theory, states are also tasked with protecting their people from themselves and each other by establishing **police forces** and **legal systems** that seek to hold members of society accountable to each other in ways that minimize social strain and maximize social stability. States also administer many of the essential **bureaucratic** aspects of social life. They mint currency, issue identification, and deliver mail, among many other tasks. Occasionally, larger groups of states will band together to form **intergovernmental organizations** such as the United Nations, European Union, or NATO. These organizations seek to pool resources and mitigate risks with the intention of lessening the burdens placed on any one state.

When the leaders of states are elected by popular vote, the systems are called **democracies**. States where a small part of the population wields state power to benefit their own interests are called authoritarian regimes and **autocracies**. Sociologists such as Max Weber have long been fascinated by the concept of **power** and the way it is used. For Weber, power represents the ability to get one's way regardless of opposition.

Power can be wielded in many different ways. **Coercion** uses fear and violence, **economic power** uses money and resources to accomplish what force might not, and **soft power** can be more subtle. One example of soft power is the use of patriotic messages or advertising embedded in popular media like movies to influence people and spread ideologies. Another example is the spread of American fast food and products throughout the world. The dominance of popular American brands and their integration into different cultural paradigms is economically motivated, but it also influences politics by affecting belief systems and encouraging those from other cultures and societies to think positively about American cultural products.

Some forms of power are attained or maintained coercively, but **authority** exists with the consent of the governed. The primary difference between power and authority is that authority—in theory—is not achieved through coercion. Members of a society grant authority to the leaders that represent them, the law enforcement agencies that police them, and the justice systems that mete out punishments, even when those institutions make decisions that might not follow their personal preferences.

Weber identified three distinct forms of authority: traditional, charismatic, and rational-legal.

WEBER'S FORMS OF AUTHORITY

Authority	Source
Traditional	Custom and history
Charismatic	Innate qualities of particularly gifted leaders
Rational-legal	Bureaucratic laws and norms that structure social and political interaction

When members of a society perceive that authority has been misused, however, they can withdraw their consent. An example of this is police violence in the United States; in many cases, people have perceived police forces utilizing power coercively and in ways that far exceed their mandated authority. Withdrawing consent from authority can take the form of **protests, social movements, political campaigns,** and even **revolutions,** which are powerful upheavals that oust a political regime in favor of one that will better reflect the populace's values and desires.

RELIGION

Religious institutions are another powerful force in shaping values and beliefs, often providing a larger cosmic context for the secular world. For many people, religious identity is as deeply ingrained as characteristics like race and ethnicity, and religious practices and traditions are important markers of identity and culture that help mediate their relationship with others. For some, religion offers hope, a sense of **cosmic** and spiritual purpose, and a community with which to share beliefs and perspectives about the world. Even those who do not identify as religious form their own sets of beliefs, values, and norms in relationship to the dominant religious perspectives in their society.

Sociologists of religion have extensively studied religious institutions and their influence on social structure. Émile Durkheim sought to strip religion down to its most basic characteristics in order to understand the elementary forms of religious life. In his studies of Indigenous cultures in Australia, he found that religious rituals can create a **collective effervescence**, a feeling of connection to an idea larger than the self. For Durkheim, who was not himself a religious person, this connection to the sacred was really the connection people had with each other and their society.

Other sociologists, such as Max Weber, sought to identify the influence that religious ideas had on social behavior. In his work on **Protestantism** in Europe and the early United States, Weber argued that the idea of predestination, coupled with the fear of not being among the select few deemed worthy of salvation, encouraged Protestants to pour their energy into their work in a way that led to significant financial success. Material wealth on earth came to be seen as a sign of divine favor; financial success proved that one had been blessed by God. Such blessings in the material world, it was hoped, would be mirrored in heavenly blessings, a thought that reassured those concerned about the status of their salvation. Weber argued that this so called "Protestant ethic" supported the continued expansion of capitalism.

Much sociological study on religious institutions has focused on **religious communities** and the places they gather. Some scholars have been interested in the question of **secularization**, or dissociation from religious beliefs and values. These sociologists study various forms of religious organization and consider whether they will persist in the future. Such scholars have studied church attendance, interviewed people from the growing population that identifies as **spiritual but not religious**, and sought to understand increasingly evident declines in religious practice and participation in the United States—a surprising result given religion's prominent role in discussions of **national identity** and politics. Other scholars study the formation of **new religions** and **cults** that follow a particularly charismatic individual leader. **Religious sects**, which are smaller offshoots of larger religious traditions, also interest scholars seeking to understand how religions organize themselves and establish orthodox beliefs and practices.

Religion and religious institutions play a powerful role in society. They can create and enforce ethical codes that encourage people to act in ways that benefit their neighbors and society. They can also, at times, be abused to exert coercive power. Because religious beliefs are often grounded in ideas of divine authority beyond mankind's understanding, they are particularly powerful tools in the hands of those interested in manipulating them to gain followers. As **religious nationalism**, religiously oriented terrorism, and the rise of cults whose members are driven to extreme and damaging behaviors show, the institution of religion can be very effectively used as a form of social control.

MEDICINE

Sociologists are also interested in the ways that medical institutions care for the **physical and mental health** of individuals in a society. Medical institutions play an important role in almost all stages of a person's life. However, the ubiquity of these institutions in everyday life does not mean that all people have equitable access to or similar experiences with them. Sociologists are also interested in how attitudes toward health care can shape people's experiences finding and receiving care for injury and illness.

In the United States, most people begin interacting with medical institutions at birth in a hospital, a birth center, or some other medical institution. Medical resources, institutions, and policies—or their lack—play an enormous role in fertility and maternal and pediatric health. However, inequalities in access, uptake, service quality, and even differences in health care workers' attitudes and training mean that maternal and infant mortality is far higher in communities of color and poor communities than in white and wealthier communities. These trends persist in all levels and stages of health care within medical institutions in the United States. There is also increasing evidence of widespread gender, sexuality, and body type bias among health care workers. Even geographic factors, such as the availability or locations of medical facilities in rural areas, can affect the access certain populations have to medical institutions.

Despite inequities in access and quality of care, medical institutions are vital for providing protection on a larger scale against disease and illness in society. However, as the COVID-19 pandemic made all too clear, these institutions are only as strong as the funding, research, and government support they receive. **Vaccine** programs, **public health** initiatives, and laws and norms regarding public behavior all shape the ability of medical institutions to respond to significant health threats. A society's **medical infrastructure** determines the extent to which these types of programs and initiatives reach the people who need them.

Medical institutions are also vital resources for supporting **mental health**, an important component of health on both personal and societal levels. Writing about the role of psychiatric institutions, French sociologist **Michel Foucault** highlighted the potential such institutions have to radically alter a person's experiences and perceptions of the world, particularly for those who are institutionalized. Modern mental health care has come a long way from the **asylums** and archaic practices Foucault analyzed, but **stigma** surrounding **mental illness** and skepticism about mental health care persist today. There is some evidence that this is changing; for example, younger generations are increasingly open about both the mental health challenges they face and the beneficial role of treatment in their lives.

The influence that medical institutions have on people's lives spans from birth to death, and the type of care and access a person has greatly influences their physical and mental health throughout life and even their experience with death. Medical institutions play a big role in **end-of-life care** and decision making, often shaping how a society deals with death and even the causes of death that are most common. Lifespans and causes of death in the United States have changed radically during the 20th and 21st centuries due to changes in medicine and medical institutions. Treatments for injuries and for illnesses such as influenza, tuberculosis, and other communicable diseases have dramatically improved, leading to far fewer deaths from these causes. However, **lifestyle diseases**, such as heart disease, lung cancer, and diabetes, have become more prominent, as have diseases such as cancer and dementia that typically occur later in life. Medical institutions like **hospice**, which offers specialized palliative end-of-life care, have developed to address the needs of a society with an increasingly older population.

CONCLUSION

Institutions are the patterns and collective organizations that shape social life. This chapter focused on some of the most important institutions, tracing how family, education, economics, politics, religion, and medicine influence structure in society and create the frameworks that govern how people live. However, these primary institutions are not the only ones:

formal organizations such as the military and the media and informal institutions such as art and culture are just a few of many other arenas in which social institutions play a role in shaping societies. At their core, institutions are the mediating organizations that structure and organize social life, but each person's experiences with these institutions are unique and vary widely depending on access, social position, and many other factors.

READINESS CHECK: INSTITUTIONS

To check how well you understand the concepts covered in this chapter, review the following questions. If you have trouble answering any of them, consider reading through this chapter again and reviewing the key terms before moving on to the next chapter.

- What role do social institutions play in preserving social stability?
- What is socialization?
- Why is family considered one of the most important institutions in a person's life?
- What is the connection between secondary agents of socialization and diversity?
- What is one primary function of education as an institution?
- What is a hidden curriculum?
- Why are economic institutions an important factor in a person's life chances?
- What is a mode of production and how does it shape a society according to Karl Marx?
- What are the four economic sectors and what do they produce?
- What is a society? A state?
- What is the difference between power and authority?
- What are the three forms of authority according to Max Weber?
- What roles do religion and religious institutions play in society?
- In what ways do people rely on medical institutions in various stages of life?

TEST YOURSELF: INSTITUTIONS

Directions: Each of the questions or incomplete statements below is followed by five suggested answers or completions. Select the one best answer for each. The Answer Key and Explanations will follow.

1. All of the following are institutions that impact social life EXCEPT

    A. elementary schools
    B. mental hospitals
    C. homes
    D. churches
    E. universities

2. Sociologists study institutions because institutions

    A. are essential elements of social theorizing
    B. are patterns of social organization that structure social life
    C. always structure economic life
    D. are Marxist representations of reality
    E. resist socialist models of society

3. Émile Durkheim's concept of organic solidarity explains

    A. social cohesion as the result of homogeneity
    B. social conflict driven by class differences
    C. the feeling of belonging driven by shared experiences of religious rituals
    D. social cohesion driven by the division of labor
    E. social disconnection driven by a reduction in religious adherence

4. Which of the following is not associated with the family as an institution?

    A. Primary socialization
    B. Marketable skills
    C. Cultural values
    D. Nuclear organization
    E. Life chances

5. Which of the following is considered the primary agent of socialization?

A. Education
B. Politics
C. Religion
D. Family
E. Economics

Answer Key and Explanations

| 1. C | 2. B | 3. D | 4. B | 5. D |

1. **The correct answer is C.** Institutions are groups or organizations founded to serve a social purpose. While family is an important social institution that impacts social life, the home itself is not considered an institution. Elementary schools (choice A) and universities (choice E) are both educational institutions, mental hospitals (choice B) are a type of medical institution, and churches (choice D) are religious institutions.

2. **The correct answer is B.** Of the options, the best summary of why scholars study institutions is that they are patterns of social organization that structure social life. Choice A is true but not unique to institutions. Choices C, D, and E are either not fully accurate or are unrelated to the question.

3. **The correct answer is D.** Durkheim's concept of organic solidarity explains the way labor is divided in a society in which people and institutions each have a particular role to play, much like how the organs within an animal each fulfill their own role. Durkheim speculated that this allowed society to function without the social homogeneity, absolute collective authority, and repressive sanctions that defined mechanical solidarity.

4. **The correct answer is B.** While a person may indeed pick up some marketable skills (choice B) from family, it is not a primary aspect of family as an institution. Primary socialization (choice A), cultural values (choice C), nuclear organization, and life chances all relate more directly to the institution of family than marketable skills do.

5. **The correct answer is D.** While each of the choices have a significant impact on socialization, the family is considered the primary agent of socialization because it is typically the first and most influential institution that a person interacts with in life.

Chapter 5

Social Patterns

OVERVIEW
- Community
- Demography
- Human Ecology and Environmental Sociology
- Rural and Urban Patterns
- Conclusion
- Readiness Check: Social Patterns
- Test Yourself: Social Patterns

When sociologists look at the world, they are often interested in social patterns—the diverse ways that people organize themselves under different circumstances. Social patterns are visible in various components of society: where people live, what their communities look like, and how people fit into the natural and social environments. Observations about these patterns tend to lead to big-picture questions about the structure and form of particular societies. Accordingly, the study of these kinds of social patterns represents 10% of the questions on the CLEP Introductory Sociology exam.

COMMUNITY

Sociology is the study of **society**. But what is society, and what distinct groups and structures comprise it? A society is a large collection of people who live together in aggregate. Societies often exist on a state- or countrywide scale. No one person can know every other person in a society; however, each person relates to others in their society as a fellow member of a group with whom they share important characteristics.

Typically operating within a society, a **community** is a type of social structure that varies in size. Some communities are small villages or neighborhoods in which the inhabitants might know or at least be familiar with all others who share the community. Other communities are cities or even midsize towns in which the inhabitants are aware of others in their area and might feel kinship with them, but they don't necessarily know other members personally. The idea of a community can also be extended beyond spatial bounds to other types of groups, such as a community of people who share an online forum dedicated to a particular topic. At their core, communities are groups of people with shared interests, cultures, beliefs, or belongings. People in communities often think of themselves as distinct in some way because of the characteristics they share. The communities a person belongs to play a key role in their daily life and the ways that they interact with others.

Many of the earliest sociologists, such as **Karl Marx, Ferdinand Tönnies,** and **Émile Durkheim,** were focused on what they perceived as the world's entrance into **modernity** and the related changes that were occurring in communal living. To these sociologists, the rise of **industrialization** and **urbanization** had created a new world in which more people were living in cities than in the small communities that had been common previously. Tönnies identified two different ways of living together. He used the German term *Gemeinschaft* to refer to the social relationships in small communities where lives overlap and members share common space and resources. He contrasted this way of living with what he called *Gesellschaft*, the impersonal social relationships in modern societies where people live separate lives and come together only in specialized roles—for example, to buy and sell goods at a market.

This change away from communal relationships represented a significant shift, and Karl Marx also identified how the transition to industrial production radically restructured social life. Marx argued that within industrialist societies, people were being reduced to tools of production instead of being valued as fully fledged human beings. This led to people experiencing **alienation**, the sense of feeling estranged from oneself, from others, and from one's work. Through the industrial transition, people also became alienated from the products their labor produced—what Marx called **alienated labor.**

Émile Durkheim, too, investigated the larger communities that developed during industrialization. Durkheim argued that modern life had separated individuals from those closest to them, isolating people from their communities and creating a sense of **anomie**, or normlessness. Without the types of deep interpersonal connections that could be found in smaller communities, Durkheim explained, each person loses their social compass, as well as their sense of how communal values and beliefs scaffold life and add meaning. Durkheim attributed a wide array of social ills to anomie, including increased rates of depression, anxiety, and suicide.

In modern sociology, communities are often objects of study for their unique characteristics. Sociologists might examine a particular neighborhood and how its residents respond to changing political situations. Alternately, they might focus on communities of shared practices rather than shared living spaces, perhaps studying a community that forms at a weekly farmers market or the shared culture that develops among fans of sports teams, particular television shows, or other cultural objects. Groups characterized by a similar race or ethnicity are sometimes referred to as communities as well based on the idea that members of these groups share distinct characteristics and systems of meaning unavailable to outsiders. For example, a community of people who have immigrated to a country share unique characteristics and experiences that cannot be easily understood by people born in that country.

What makes communities distinct, however, can also lead to social inequalities. The conditions of one community may differ from another, and **social stratification** can mean that members of one community may have opportunities or challenges that others may not. Sociologists often keep potential inequalities in mind, paying close attention to the things that distinguish life lived in one community from that lived in another. Chapter 7 discusses the ways sociologists address social stratification in more depth.

Some sociologists work closely with communities in practice-based settings as a form of activism or social justice work. Today, the term **community sociology** can refer to the work of sociologists who embed themselves in a community and take a practical, hands-on approach to solving social problems. Professionals in allied fields such as social work, counseling, and community organization are in many ways community sociologists as well. The goal of these practitioners is to intervene directly in the social conditions of a community, a much more action-based approach than that taken by sociologists.

DEMOGRAPHY

For any sort of sociological research, it is important to have an accurate understanding of a population's characteristics. To accomplish this task,

sociologists ask themselves multiple questions:
- Who is a member of this society?
- What attributes do they share?
- In what ways is the population diverse?

The statistical study of populations is referred to as **demography**. Demographers play a significant role in mapping out various dimensions of social life, including age, gender, race, marital status, occupation, income, education level, and more.

Many demographers draw their data from large-scale surveys such as censuses, comprehensive government records, or other similar efforts to gather data across a wide swath of society. Most surveys include questions designed to gather demographic data, and institutions such as medical offices and schools also ask a range of demographic questions that help them assess their successes and failures and ascertain whether there are any inequalities in outcomes across demographic groups. **Formal demographics** involves the study of population processes, including data on birth and death rates, population growth, and migration. **Social demographics** broaden the area of focus to include other sorts of statistics such as race, gender, and social class.

Demographers analyze population dynamics because such figures provide valuable information about the direction in which a society is headed. For example, birth and death rates provide insights into whether a population is growing or shrinking over time. In Europe, Japan, the United States, and other wealthier and technologically developed countries, birth rates have been decreasing for decades. By examining social demographics, sociologists have determined that this decline is the result of increasing levels of education and better access to birth control and family planning. Women in these societies are increasingly able to choose when or if they have children and how many children they wish to have. Women entering the workplace may choose to delay having children until their careers are established or forego having children at all. Changes such as these are reflections of increased freedom and opportunity; however, according to some sociologists, declining birth rates may be cause for alarm. More reproductive choice means fewer children, and when birth rates drop below death rates, a society may begin to shrink in a way that ultimately affects its future structure and social dynamics. Concerns over shrinking populations have led some countries, such as Japan, to offer incentives for having children.

However, other demographic phenomena also play a role. Better technology and increased access to health care have led to increases in average life expectancy in many wealthy countries. This has allowed people to live and work far longer than previous generations, stalling the effects of certain demographic changes. Yet here, too, challenges lurk. Some experts have identified the scenario in which older members of society outnumber younger generations, sometimes referred to as a "**gray wave**," as problematic. For instance, the large population of baby boomers (i.e., those born between approximately 1946 and 1964) in the United States, themselves the product of shifting demographics at the end of World War II, continue to age and are beginning to require increased medical care. Some project that the younger generations who have followed may not have the resources or workforce necessary to care for this aging population, creating a social burden that may prove challenging to overcome.

It's important to note that these types of challenges exist almost exclusively in technologically developed countries. Elsewhere, other societies face different dilemmas. In parts of Africa and south and central Asia, the issue is reversed: birth rates are extremely high, and prevalent poverty levels mean that resources are spread thin. High birth rates can exponentially increase populations; if more people are born in one generation, then more people are reproducing in the next. If birth rates stay high, the following generations become even larger. In many ways, birth rates and wealth are interconnected. Just as increasing wealth and education have given people options in countries like the United States, poverty and poor education systems—along with other factors, including the legacy of colonialism and corrupt and ineffective governments—have limited the options and life chances of people in other countries.

This dichotomy between the experiences of technologically developed and developing countries has led some countries to turn to migration as a possible solution to demographic challenges. Some countries with low birth rates rely on those with higher rates as a source of labor. Other countries have deliberately made themselves exporters of labor, building large parts of their economy around sending workers abroad to meet the needs of wealthier societies. This situation seems to be an equitable exchange: countries with money but fewer workers contract with countries who have less money but a surplus of workers to balance out patterns of demographic changes. While this can be the case at times, it is also a situation with complicated dynamics that can result in the exploitation of laborers, especially those with few other options. Organized human trafficking, exploitation of undocumented populations, and anti-immigrant sentiments in many parts of the world are just a few challenges faced by those seeking work abroad.

These examples represent a few of the ways that demographic change can affect what a society looks like. They also illustrate how seemingly uncomplicated raw data such as birth and death rates, statistics on aging, and immigration data can lead to controversy and political divides. Demographers trace these sorts of patterns because they matter to the development and function of society. Understanding the population dynamics of a society and the ways those dynamics change are critically important for sociologists hoping to understand social behaviors and the causes of social problems.

HUMAN ECOLOGY AND ENVIRONMENTAL SOCIOLOGY

The study of human populations in and of themselves is important, but some sociologists have turned their attention to the ways human societies fit in with and affect the natural world. Within the field of sociology, studies of the relationship between humans and the environment can take two primary forms: human ecology and environmental sociology.

Human Ecology

Human ecology is a field that draws from a variety of social and natural sciences to assess how people and societies interact with the environment. Human ecologists look at human beings as a total population, and they use their research to deepen their understanding of the ecology—the habitats, social structures, and relationships—common to different societies.

The study of human ecology owes much to the study of natural ecology, a field of science that studies relationships between organisms and their environment. A natural ecologist, for example, might look at different animal populations in a pond and its environs, exploring how beavers shape the natural structure of the pond, how fish and frogs compete for insects as food, and how life patterns vary seasonally as temperatures shift and water levels rise and fall. Similarly, human ecologists examine the relationships of humans to their environment. Human ecologists might ask questions like the following:

- How do humans construct homes?
- How do humans arrange their workplaces?
- What factors do humans consider when creating public buildings?
- What do processes of food production look like, and what type of infrastructure is necessary for people to be comfortably fed?

Answers to questions like these differ from population to population and society to society. Human ecologists may isolate their study to a particular region and/or time period, but they are ultimately trying to relate that work to more universal human tendencies.

Let's consider the question about food production and investigate how a human ecologist might approach it. Human food production is a complicated process that relies on many interconnected infrastructures. Today, humans produce food far differently than they did 200 years ago, let alone 2,000 years ago, and collective social patterns have shifted as a result. No longer do all people need to farm, hunt, and gather food to maintain a minimal level of subsistence. With a food surplus, people can do different jobs that did not exist in the past—as mechanics, politicians, accountants, and sociologists, for example—and continue to improve food systems. Both adaptation to the environment and better technology have drastically changed how humans produce food.

A similar investigation could be made into the first two questions about how humans construct the buildings in which they live and work. A sociologist in human ecology might study how different environments in the United States necessitate different structures. For example, buildings in California are earthquake proofed, a reaction to the natural setting in which Californians live. Conversely, houses in Galveston, Texas, and many coastal parts of Florida are constructed on stilts to help avoid damage from storm surges produced by seasonal hurricanes. In the Midwest and Northeast, buildings are constructed to protect people from colder temperatures, while in Arizona and other parts of the Southwest, buildings are designed to shed heat and capture cool breezes to combat extreme summer temperatures.

These types of research help sociologists understand how human populations fit into the world. No matter how technologically advanced societies become, humans operate within the natural world and must consider how to interact with environmental challenges and phenomena.

Environmental Sociology

Environmental sociology builds on the types of questions asked by human ecology but turns its focus to the ways that the relationship between humans and their environment is mutually constitutive: environments affect how humans act and structure their societies, but human populations have a dramatic impact on the natural world as well. Humans have always altered their environment but have done so on a vastly larger scale since the Industrial Revolution of the 19th century. The switch to heavy industry and mass production, and especially the use of fossil fuels, has shifted the ways humans use natural resources. The consumption of fuels such as coal and oil has produced greenhouse gases in immense quantities, enough to alter natural environments. Research suggests these changes have led to **anthropogenic climate change**, widescale measurable changes to the climate caused by human activity.

Other human-led environmental changes such as the damming of rivers, increased plowing of land for agricultural purposes, and deforestation also have had significant impacts on the natural world. Environmental sociologists study these changes, as well as how anthropogenic climate and environmental changes impact the people who experience their effects.

Environmental sociologists study the ways climate change and other natural disasters affect different populations. Poorer populations are often affected at higher rates by climate and environmental change than wealthier populations for a variety of reasons. Wealthier people may be able to afford to build or buy houses in more desirable areas, further away from potentially dangerous natural disaster zones. They may also be able to relocate when a situation becomes environmentally untenable, a drought occurs, or repeated storms damage homes and infrastructure, and they can rebuild, when necessary, with greater ease than those with fewer resources. Moreover, wealthier populations can exert more influence on policymakers, including those who allocate disaster funding or determine where high-pollution plants or factories will be built. In contrast, poorer communities often have few, if any, resources for addressing structural and systemic issues, leaving them to simply endure climate shifts and environmental change.

Environmental sociologists expect that human-caused environmental changes will not only continue to affect the world but will also worsen over time. The damage caused by extreme weather events and other effects of climate change have led people to react accordingly. Contemporary sociologists have noted a rise in climate-related migration and an increase in the number of **climate refugees**, people who have fled their homes in response to changing weather patterns.

Environmental sociologists have also sought to focus attention on the types of climate inequalities they observe in the world. To this end, one branch of environmental sociology is invested in **climate justice**, the idea that by working to mitigate the effects of climate change for the most vulnerable populations, humans can create a more equitable global society in which the burdens of a changing climate are shared equally by all.

RURAL AND URBAN PATTERNS

One area of interest for human ecologists and environmental sociologists alike is the question of where people live, which is a key component in the study of social patterns. Sociologists are interested in understanding how the distribution of people in terms of physical location affects the composition of a society. One key distinction that some scholars have focused on is the difference between **rural** and **urban** locations in patterns of social life.

Humans are social creatures. As such, it is human nature to form communities and common areas for social living. Communities take many shapes and forms, from densely populated cities like New York City or Tokyo, to similarly large but sprawling cities such as Los Angeles or Istanbul, to small villages scattered throughout rural areas, with a variety of midsized **suburban** towns in between. Sociologists interested in patterns of human habitation often focus on this diversity, investigating the ways life is different in large urban areas and small rural areas, and why, exactly, a person might choose to live in one or the other.

Rural Communities

The earliest recorded societies were **rural communities**. By definition, rural communities are small in size and their population density and settlement patterns are based on the terrain and occupation of the inhabitants. Rural communities are dependent on natural resources and often based on an agrarian economy, although forestry, mining, or fishery may also be the primary industry. Rural areas tend to be homogenous societies with many residents engaged in similar occupations. Often, farms and businesses—and their corresponding trade skills—are passed down through families for generations. In many regions, social stratification based on age, gender, or caste is also a traditional characteristic.

However, the long-standing social and economic structures of rural societies have not been immune to the effects of technology and industrialization. For example, in recent years, some rural communities in the United States have served as labor resources for manufacturing plants, which helped to augment the base economy. Over time, industry relocation and outsourcing resulted in widespread unemployment and poverty in many of these areas. Additionally, the growing trend of young people moving to urban areas has also had a negative impact on such communities.

Today, rural living may be the choice of people seeking reduced pollution, access to healthier food, a stronger sense of community, lower crime rates and stress levels, and more space. Those who seek such advantages are willing to accept potential disadvantages such as poor infrastructure, lack of public transportation, reduced shopping and entertainment options, reduced career opportunities, and limited access to modern health care. Sociologists study these factors alongside broader economic and social trends to better understand social structures in rural areas.

Urban Areas

Some of the early sociologists of the 19th century critically studied what they observed as society's transition to modernity. Mass production and other forms of industrial advancement had shifted the division of labor, upending traditional social patterns as people flocked to cities (centers of production) and away from rural areas. In their own ways, Marx, Tönnies, and Durkheim each argued that city life brought with it changing social conditions and that these new conditions were potentially damaging to the lives and psyches of people as they were incorporated into the economic and social patterns of urban life.

The Industrial Revolution had a significant impact on urbanization, both due to the growth of large cities and the change in demographics as a growing proportion of the population began living in urban rather than rural environments. Despite this acceleration in urban living, many large cities predated modernity. Urban environments such as Uruk, Thebes, Rome, Chang'an, and Tenochtitlan grew to immense scales at various points in history. These early cities were important centers of culture and economic life, but for much of history, large cities were exceedingly rare.

Even in antiquity, cities acted as core economic and production zones around which rural agricultural space could be found. Food and other raw materials would be produced or gathered in the outskirts of cities and transported to the city center for consumption. Some scholars study cities through this lens of consumption-based domination, describing them as **consumption cities** in contrast to cities that are sites of production. Others emphasize the complicated interplay of social and economic ties between urban and rural areas and look at the ways they support each other through mutual production.

Today, however, for the first time in human history, most people in the world live in urban areas. The growth of urban environments has created the world's first **megacities**, urban agglomerations of 10 million or more people, and **global cities**, places whose influence extends far beyond national and continental boundaries. Such urban settings are where most human population growth is expected to take place in the near future. The exponential nature of birth rates, where they remain high, means that the percentage of people living in cities will continue to grow, while other changes, such as climate disasters or shifting economic patterns, may encourage even more people to migrate to urban areas.

Rapid urbanization since the Industrial Revolution has brought with it myriad problems. Higher population densities in urban centers can lead to greater demands and increased competition for resources. Such factors can create inequalities that lead to, among other problems, the growth of **slums**, vast urban areas with few resources where the increasing number of residents have limited options for work and few resources to support themselves. *Favelas* in Brazil, *gecekondular* in Turkey, and makeshift shanty towns elsewhere in the world reveal the consequences of increased urbanization without adequate urban planning and social support. Even in wealthy countries, such as the United States, some urban areas lack consistent access to clean water and often contain areas known as **food deserts**—typically defined as low-income areas where residents lack convenient and/or affordable access to fresh or nutritional foods.

Meanwhile, advances in telecommunications technology have allowed some urban dwellers to be able to work from home rather than in traditional workplace settings. This has meant that some people, albeit mostly white-collar workers, have been able to move out of urban environments and live in suburban and rural settings while continuing to work in the same positions that once required urban living. Such demographic shifts can be compounded by the outsourcing of jobs to other countries offering cheaper labor. Workforce changes like these affect income distribution and influence political decisions about infrastructure spending and social support, all with the potential to affect the quality of urban living.

Urban revitalization efforts seek to rehabilitate urban life through investment in real estate, rezoning, and community areas. However, such projects risk exacerbating **gentrification**, a process by which investment in an area raises the cost of living such that it becomes too expensive for long-time inhabitants, forcing many to move out or, in worst case scenarios, lose housing entirely. These consequences highlight how challenging it can be to work for social change in a neighborhood or community or even on a citywide level. Efforts to improve the quality of life in cities risk driving out the people who live in them.

Urban patterns continue to shift, responding slowly but decisively to changes in demographics, technology, economics, and politics in the modern world. Sociologists continue to watch and analyze these changes to better understand the directions societies are heading and the conditions under which people will live now and in the future.

CONCLUSION

This chapter has discussed patterns of human social life, emphasizing the importance of large-scale population processes and the ways sociologists study them. The communities in which people live play a powerful role in shaping everyday life, as do the natural and built environments in which everyday life occurs. Sociologists and demographers study these patterns to better understand how humans live and the key characteristics that shape people's lives. Whether in urban environments or rural areas, a person's surroundings shape their experiences and the options available to them—a key component in the sociological study of social patterns.

READINESS CHECK: SOCIAL PATTERNS

To check how well you understand the concepts covered in this chapter, review the following questions. If you have trouble answering any of them, consider reading through this chapter again and reviewing the key terms before moving on to the next chapter.

- What is a society? What is a community? How are the two terms different?
- What is *Gemeinschaft*? *Gesellschaft*? What early sociologist is responsible for defining these terms?
- What does the term *alienation* mean in Marx's theories?
- What is anomie? Who defined the term? How is it related to industrialization and urbanization, and what effect can it have on individuals?
- What is demography? What are the differences between formal and social demographics?
- What is the relationship between human ecology and environmental sociology?
- Why is the study of urban versus rural areas of particular interest to sociologists?
- What is gentrification? Why is it a concern for sociologists who study urbanization?

TEST YOURSELF: SOCIAL PATTERNS

Directions: Each of the questions or incomplete statements below is followed by five suggested answers or completions. Select the one best answer for each. The Answer Key and Explanations will follow.

1. Demography refers to the statistical study of

   A. democracy
   B. human populations
   C. political agitators
   D. human/environment interactions
   E. community-based activism

2. Which of the following would NOT be the type of project a human ecologist might undertake?

   A. An analysis of how architectural styles in various regions take environmental concerns into account
   B. Research exploring traffic patterns in major metro areas to help policymakers decide where to build a new highway
   C. An examination of how increasing drought patterns in some parts of the world have caused people to migrate to wetter climates
   D. An ethnographic analysis of a religious community studying opinions about the afterlife
   E. An examination of the cultural effects of gentrification in communities within large North American cities historically populated by minorities

3. Ferdinand Tönnies sought to understand differences in community organization, arguing that premodern communities operated under conditions of _____ while modern communities had transitioned to _____ .

   A. *Gesellschaft ... Gemeinschaft*
   B. ruralism ... urbanism
   C. *Gemeinschaft ... Gesellschaft*
   D. anomie ... capitalism
   E. egalitarianism ... stratification

4. Scholars trace the increase in urbanism in the modern world to

   A. industrial development that creates an increased need for a labor force concentrated in one location

   B. social psychological processes that have led people to feel closer to each other and thus to desire living in closer proximity

   C. social policy changes, changes in social attitudes, and the transformation of gender roles

   D. disenchantment with traditional forms of religion that has discouraged communing with nature in rural settings

   E. changes in food production that make urban gardening more profitable than rural agriculture

5. Brayan lives in an apartment building in a working-class and racially diverse neighborhood within a large urban center. Since Brayan moved into the neighborhood, several small businesses, including coffee shops, art galleries, and bars, have opened. Additionally, some of the older buildings in the neighborhood have been torn down to make room for newer luxury apartment buildings. When Brayan meets with his landlord to renew his lease, he learns that his monthly rent will be increased by hundreds of dollars. Brayan's neighborhood is most likely experiencing

   A. urbanization

   B. gentrification

   C. suburbanization

   D. urban sprawl

   E. white flight

Answer Key and Explanations

1. B	2. D	3. C	4. A	5. B

1. **The correct answer is B.** Demographers examine population dynamics in various human populations, examining both formal and social demographics, including age, gender, race, marital status, occupation, income, and education level.

2. **The correct answer is D.** An ethnographic analysis entails an immersive, in-depth observation of a community or culture, which would not be the focus of a human ecology project. Analysis of architectural styles (choice A), research into traffic patterns (choice B), and an examination of the effects of drought patterns on migration (choice C) or gentrification on community culture (choice E) all study human interaction with built and natural environments—the ecological niches humans construct for themselves.

3. **The correct answer is C.** *Gemeinschaft* refers to premodern communal bonds while *Gesellschaft* describes modern social bonds in societies where people live more individualized lives and come together only for specific purposes. Choice A has the terms reversed. The terms in the remaining answer choices all describe a pair of opposing community lifestyles, but only choice C correctly identifies the terms Tönnies coined in the proper order.

4. **The correct answer is A.** Scholars as early as Marx point to how technological and industrial change have shifted patterns of labor use. More labor is needed for mass industry in urban environments and more efficient agriculture techniques have reduced the size of the workforce needed to produce a surplus of food in rural environments.

5. **The correct answer is B.** Gentrification occurs when the investment in an urban area, usually an affordable neighborhood within a city, increases the cost of living for existing residents of that area, pricing them out of their own neighborhood. This process usually involves the creation of businesses that appeal to people with more disposable income as well as the construction of new housing to encourage people to move to the neighborhood, driving up the cost of living, especially rent payments. None of the other choices match each aspect of the situation described in the question.

Chapter 6

Social Processes

OVERVIEW
- Social Interaction
- Culture
- Socialization
- Deviance and Social Control
- Social Change
- Collective Behavior and Social Movements
- Groups and Organizations
- Conclusion
- Readiness Check: Social Processes
- Test Yourself: Social Processes

Sociologists focus on **social processes** because they are the core sets of interactions and behaviors through which people establish the structures, rules, and norms that help hold societies together. Social processes teach people how to behave, what is expected of them, and what penalties to expect for deviating from the behavior that society has deemed best. Social processes often create patterns to compel people to follow sets of behaviors, but some social processes are designed to challenge the norms and expectations of society. These kinds of processes help build movements and mobilize support to effect social change. Given their central role in the study of social behavior, social processes are the subject of 25% of the questions on the CLEP Introductory Sociology examination.

SOCIAL INTERACTION

Social interaction is at the heart of a wide range of social processes. One of the core tenets of sociology is that humans are social creatures. People organize themselves into social groups for a wide range of reasons, and it is social interaction that makes any form of society or social group possible. In many ways, sociology is the study of social interaction—sociologists examine how interactions between people create the **social patterns** and **social structures** on which complex social worlds are built.

Sociologists study social interaction in many forms and on many **levels of analysis**. Some sociologists are interested in the microlevel patterns of individual interaction in discrete moments of contact, a type of sociology called **microsociology**. Sociologists who practice **conversation analysis**, for example, pay close attention to word choice in everyday life with consideration of the time and place of the utterance. For example, a sociologist studying a situation in which a police officer pulls someone over on the road might ask a variety of questions. What procedures does the officer follow? What formal language and patterns of behavior does the officer use to confront someone who would rather avoid a ticket or other legal sanctions? Conversely, how does the civilian respond in a roadside police encounter? What might lead someone to accept a ticket quietly, and what might encourage them to argue? How might race, gender, or other identity markers factor into the word choices either party uses? What are the patterns of behavior on either side that might lead to an escalation of tensions such that the confrontation leads to violence? The sociologist is interested in what the answers to these questions reveal about social interaction at its most basic level.

Other sociologists are more interested in large-scale patterns of social interaction, a type of sociology called **macrosociology**. These sociologists might be interested in questions about groups of people in a wide range of circumstances. What might lead people to join a group **protest**? What are the circumstances necessary for a **political revolution** to occur in a particular country? In what significant ways has social interaction expanded in the internet age that previously would have been impossible or would have taken more time? These large-scale social processes of governmental change, **social revolution**, and global technological changes are also the products of social interaction.

CULTURE

Some types of social interactions lead to the creation of phenomena called **cultures**. While the word *culture* in the English language holds a wide variety of definitions and uses in everyday speech, in sociology, it describes the norms and behaviors that a particular group of people share. These norms can incorporate elements from a range of **practices**, including **belief systems, arts, customs, ideologies, interests**, and ways of understanding the world. Sometimes scholars use the concept of culture as a way to describe distinct divisions between discrete groups of people, often associating a culture with a particular country or region of the world. People tend to understand, for example, that being French is different from being Nigerian, both of which are also different from being Peruvian. While these terms indicate differences in nationality, they also indicate differences in culture, language, and various other characteristics that distinguish each group from other groups or cultures.

On closer examination, however, these objective distinctions become more complicated. It's likely that the culture or group described as French shares some characteristics, but what precisely are the characteristics of someone who does or does not fit within this category? Does it mean being born in the territory called France? What about someone born to French parents living abroad? Does it mean speaking the French language? If so, how French is a first-year university student whose connection to French culture is limited to a foreign language requirement? What about the large population of French-speaking inhabitants of formerly colonized countries around the world?

Perhaps being French means a genetic connection to the inhabitants of the country of France. Here, too, things are complicated. How connected must someone be? And at what point do descendants living outside of France stop being French? Some sociologists have defaulted to considering social forms of culture such as these to be voluntary, requiring a commitment to the ideas and norms of a culture. But does that mean anyone can belong to any culture if they just believe it enough?

These types of dilemmas show exactly how hard it is to pin down the concept of culture. It's a loose set of characteristics that may or may not entirely connote membership in a community. Some of these are **ascribed characteristics** while others are **achieved characteristics**; that is, some are things people are born with while others are characteristics they acquire over a lifetime of learning. Moving the framework away from national or **anthropological** types of culture to other forms allows sociologists to study how these collections of cultural characteristics operate in people's daily lives.

Looking within national communities, rather than between them, sociologists find other cultural distinctions. **Popular culture** encompasses an array of cultural components, diverse markets, and identities that are theoretically accessible to all. A person can be a fan of a sports team, a television show, or a particular music artist and belong to a community of fans with few barriers to entry or participation. Popular culture, by definition, is broadly accessible. Other forms of culture are more difficult to access. **Elite** or **high culture** require different levels of **social capital** and **cultural capital** to access. Money and high **economic class** often play a significant role; events and experiences that are important in elite culture are often priced out of the reach of the rest of society.

However, money is only one part of what allows an individual to associate with elite culture; **taste** is also required, meaning a knowledge of what is and what is not appropriate for someone of that elite status to enjoy. For example, in the United States, a Broadway play and a NASCAR race will attract different audiences. Each audience's cultural background, as well as social pressures regarding the types of cultural products that members of a given social class ought to like, might make one type of entertainment more accessible and interesting to one group than another.

In his groundbreaking book *Distinction*, sociologist **Pierre Bourdieu** made a detailed study of taste and how it differs between elite and non-elite segments of society. Bourdieu's study revealed that networks of social connections with other elites and markers of elite identity, such as membership in specific social clubs or degrees from elite educational institutions, serve as additional markers of belonging in high-culture circles. Consider the differences between the King of England and a recent lottery winner or a rock star, for instance. All three individuals may possess comparable **economic capital**, but other forms of social and cultural distinction play a role in identity and belonging.

The ubiquity of popular culture and the exclusionary nature of high culture have led many people to form groups that distinguish themselves from societal norms. These groups are defined depending on the degree of departure from societal expectations. Smaller groups that exist within society, under the umbrella of broader cultural norms, are **subcultures**. Groups that define themselves in opposition to societal norms dictating what is right and proper are **countercultures**. In countering mainstream culture, these groups create cultures in and of themselves. Ironically, these groups may share a distaste for the popular and "normal" and yet create a whole set of (countercultural) norms and behaviors of their own. Punks, goths, hipsters, and other groups in the United States have all defined themselves with symbols and norms that distinguish but don't fully separate them from traditional values, making them good examples of subcultures. A relatively globalized counterculture developed during the 1960s when the civil rights and antiwar movements and the Beat movement sought to change the prevailing culture of the time.

SOCIALIZATION

Social and cultural understanding are not just products of natural human drives; they are the result of each individual's lifelong process of learning how to fit in and trying to understand the social rules and expectations required of them in any given group or situation. Sociologists refer to this learning process as **socialization**, and it is responsible for the development of people's personalities and their ability to exist in a social world. Scholars have long been interested in the question of **nature versus nurture**: How much of behavior and personality is innate and how much is taught to people through processes of social learning? Sociologists place heavy emphasis on the idea that social groups are deeply important to this development process. There are many types of **socializers**, and people become socialized to changing situations throughout their lives. However, scholars have identified some particularly important socializers and traced the contributions they make to people's lives. Many of the socialization functions that institutions play are discussed in Chapter 4.

Families are the first **socializing agents**. They shape people's first experiences with the world and teach many of the fundamentals of being human. For this reason, sociologists call the family a primary agent of socialization. Families teach foundational skills, such as how to feed and dress oneself, and patterns of behavior that allow people to eventually join social life. Families also teach language and the values and ideals of the community and culture. Families are especially powerful socializers for two reasons: people spend most of their time with their family as young children, and families have a vested interest in children's learning and experiences.

As children grow, so too do the number of socialization agents in their lives. Early education and formal schooling play key roles, acting as secondary agents of socialization. **Schools** develop a new set of skills necessary for success in society. They can teach not only the basics of academic subjects that will be useful in future societal roles, but they can also prepare young people for the everyday business of being an adult. More than that, however, schools teach children about a world beyond the family. Children are likely to encounter **diversity** for the first time as they learn that other people may not share the cultural characteristics of their own families. They also start to learn ways of behaving in public: how to sit still, follow a schedule, obey authority figures, collaborate, and exist in settings in which they are not the center of attention. Moreover, spending much of the day at school helps children develop a sense of identity that is separate from any expectations their families may have set for them.

For similar reasons, **peer groups** also become more important as people leave the home and function in society. Peer groups teach things that formal institutions such as schools might not. They can reinforce ideas of what is and isn't "cool." They can teach people ways of fitting in with those around them or the informal rules that govern peer-to-peer interactions. Unlike family and schooling, people have a degree of choice about their peer groups and come to learn what characteristics they prefer in friends and colleagues. They also learn who they don't enjoy spending time with and how to break ties with those people. Often, sociologists think of peer groups as socializers that expose people to new ideas. Exposure does not ensure adoption, but such socializers can encourage people to ignore or disregard the messages taught to them by families and schools. Just because families believe one thing, for example, doesn't mean their children will (or have to) believe the same thing. As socialization continues, people learn about new options and ideas from the people they meet as they form peer groups. Young people might learn "bad" behaviors, such as skipping school, or they might learn to resist authority to counter a perceived injustice.

Beyond immediate peers, **mass media** and **social media** are important socialization agents. Media exposes people to contexts beyond their own immediate social settings, illustrating that the world contains far more diversity than what is often displayed in their own hometowns or peer groups. People can learn about national and international **trends**, be influenced to behave in certain ways, purchase certain things, and find social and cultural niches that may not have been available in their immediate environments.

Other socializers play different types of roles in people's lives. Organizations, governments, and religions all act as socializing agents in both narrow and broad contexts. For example, people are taught how to act in their professional lives by their jobs. Expectations and behaviors may change when they change employment or careers. Those who join the military or other structured institutions also undergo specific socialization processes. Through basic training, an individual learns what is expected of a soldier in defense of their country. Those who observe religious practices are often socialized by their observance, and those norms can be followed broadly or only in specific contexts. The widespread nature of socialization means that people continually learn new ways of acting and being, encounter new expectations, and develop new assumptions about proper behavior throughout their lives.

DEVIANCE AND SOCIAL CONTROL

No matter how strong socializing processes are, no one acts entirely in accord with the expectations society places on them. Anyone who has ever driven over the speed limit, stayed out after curfew, or dressed out of step with expected social conventions has participated in what sociologists call **deviance**. Deviance refers to straying in some way, even if very small, from the social and cultural **norms** of society. In the United States, deviance carries negative connotations. However, from a sociological perspective, deviance is not inherently negative. People can practice **positive deviance**, going above and beyond society's expectations of them. Martin Luther King Jr., Mahatma Gandhi, Mother Theresa, Malala Yousafzai, and other figures are considered to be models of great moral standing for violating the norms of their respective societies, and they are considered deviant by sociological standards.

But deviance, even positive deviance, is often looked down on by society. Deviance involves a difference from the norm, and societies are invested in maintaining the **status quo** because change and difference often threaten social stability, for good or for ill. For this reason, people encounter **social sanctions**, which can include rewards for appropriate behavior and penalties for inappropriate behavior from institutions and the people around them. **Positive sanctions** seek to reward appropriate behavior, whether with a simple "thank you" or a material prize. **Negative sanctions** can take a variety of forms, including **informal** social shunning and mockery. Depending on the nature of the deviant act, more **formal** legal sanctions may occur, such as criminal penalties, imprisonment, or even execution.

Like socialization itself, social sanctions are a form of social control; they are used to enforce adherence to social norms. From a societal perspective, social sanctions and pushback against deviance encourage people to act in a way deemed beneficial to society to prevent a dissolution into anarchy. Only through **conformity** and collective buy-in to social norms and behaviors can society ensure its continued coherence and relevance. Social sanctions assure that anyone threatening that structure and stability is gently, and then increasingly firmly, pressured into alignment with society, in turn strengthening social norms.

SOCIAL CHANGE

Social change is a significant alteration of social norms and is the result of various factors. Through the process of social change, subcultures can be created, or the major culture of a society can be altered. In the United States, examples of significant social changes with long-term effects include the abolition of slavery; the Industrial Revolution; the civil rights, feminist, and LGBTQ+ rights movements; and the environmentalism movement of the 1960s.

Types of Social Change

Sociologists categorize social change into two main forms: **evolutionary social change**, which happens as a natural result of societal trends; and **revolutionary social change**, which is a sudden, complete, or drastic change from previous social norms. Catalysts for social change include the following:

- **Conflicts:** social movements and marginalized groups challenging existing power structures
- **Cultural changes:** technological and communication innovations, scientific discoveries, and the sharing of ideas
- **Demographic changes:** fluctuations in birth and death rates, population shifts, or new migration patterns
- **Institutional changes:** shifts in economic, political, or religious institutions
- **Environmental changes:** negative changes to the environment (natural or human-caused) and social or interest group intervention or calls to action

These causes often affect each other or can combine to create larger social change.

Models of Social Change

To understand the nature of long-term social change, sociologists examine historical data, looking for patterns and causes through the lens of one of three models of social change: evolutionary, functionalist, or conflict theory.

According to **evolutionary theory**, society changes from simple to more complex levels. Early social evolutionists, such as **August Comte** and **Hebert Spencer**, believed that society gradually progressed to higher levels of organization. As such, they concluded that their own cultural attitudes and behaviors were more advanced than those of previous societies. Comte's **unilinear evolutionary theory** proposed that all societies pass through the same stages and paths of evolution to ultimately reach the same level of advancement. However, contemporary social evolutionists like **Gerhard Lenski Jr.** believe social change can evolve along different lines in varied ways and does not inevitably lead in the same direction, a perspective called **multilinear evolutionary theory**.

Functionalist theory focuses not on what changes society but what maintains it. According to Talcott Parsons's **equilibrium theory,** society naturally moves toward a state of **homeostasis**; thus, significant social problems, such as labor strikes, represent nothing but temporary rifts in the social order. Parsons posited that changes in one part of society require adjustments in other parts. When these adjustments do not occur, equilibrium disappears, and social order is threatened. While Parsons's equilibrium theory embraces the concept of continuing progress supported by evolutionary theory, its prevalent theme is maintaining balance and stability.

Conflict theory, as posited by **Karl Marx**, maintains that change plays a vital role in remedying the social inequalities and injustices inherent in capitalism. These injustices are a result of the wealthy and powerful striving to ensure that social practices and institutions favorable to them continue. Thus, only through revolution will exploitation of the working class be eliminated from society, making conflict both desirable and necessary in order to initiate social change.

COLLECTIVE BEHAVIOR AND SOCIAL MOVEMENTS

When individuals violate social norms, they are considered deviant, but when enough individuals challenge the same norms in an organized fashion, they constitute a **social movement**. Social movements arise when people identify **social problems**—specific issues in the world with which they are dissatisfied.

One unhappy person rarely has the power to change the world. More commonly, people struggling with particular social issues may come to realize that others share their concerns and struggles. This sense of shared struggle can form the foundation for **social action**. Though an individual rarely has the power to change social situations single-handedly, enough people working together can exert influence far beyond what they could as individuals.

To create and grow a social movement, political activists and those hoping to effect change must **mobilize** support, gathering a critical mass of people willing to join the movement. This is easier said than done, however, as there are significant barriers to mobilization. **Inertia**, social pressures, and the challenge of the **free rider problem**, in which some people benefit from a collective effort without contributing to it themselves, all make social movements more difficult to establish and maintain.

To mobilize support for a movement, **activists** often create a **frame**, that is, a particular way of speaking about an issue to encourage people to support the cause. The struggle around reproductive rights in the United States, for example, is often framed as a debate between pro-choice and pro-life movements. Both are ways of thinking about an issue through a particular ideological lens.

As part of the framing process, social movement activists also work to establish **grounds, warrants,** and **conclusions**. These are essential elements that define an issue. Grounds are evidence that there is a problem. Activists strive to point out social issues, sometimes by using specific examples or by discussing social harms. Once an issue is sufficiently defined, activists work to establish its warrants—concerted arguments that people should be invested in the issue and should be responsible for taking action to solve it. Conclusions are statements about what should be done and the strategy the activists hope to take. Action is important, but concerted action using one established set of tactics to achieve one particular set of goals is essential for creating social change.

Significant changes have come about as the result of social movements. The labor movement, civil rights movement, and the women's liberation movement are all examples of fruitful social movements in the United States. Social movements can be effective, but their effects are not always immediate. Social movements are always pushing against established **social structures** and the status quo, and they often also spark **countermovements**, in which those invested in the current system react against the prospect of social change and assert their desire to maintain the status quo. Nevertheless, the strength of people working in tandem toward a particular goal has the potential to effect dramatic changes in a society.

GROUPS AND ORGANIZATIONS

Sociologists studying collective action must pay attention to the patterns of relationships within a society. This field of study is called the sociology of **groups** or, when such groups are more formally structured, **organizations**. This area of sociology is interested in why people organize, what benefits people get from joining groups, how and why such groups operate, and where people draw the boundaries between those in the group and those outside. Organizational studies are interested in how and why organizations are structured in certain ways and how those organizational structures influence daily life.

The term *group* refers to any collection of people who share a particular characteristic in common and take action to emphasize that characteristic, viewing people who share it as in some way different from others. Group membership often brings with it a sense of **belonging** and the idea that being a part of such a group constitutes an **identity**, or a distinguishing characteristic that separates some people from others. Groups can be formed across many dimensions, in everything from **ethnicity** or **religion** to informal groups of choice (e.g., friendships, fandoms, shared interest groups, etc.).

Some scholars have posited that humans are socially inclined to think in terms of groups. **Émile Durkheim**, for instance, examined the collective effervescence that comes from shared participation in social groups. Others have been interested in where groups begin and end—how someone is identified as being part of a particular **in-group** or **out-group**—and what that means for human relationships. Some scholars have cautioned against overemphasizing the power of groupness since a shared sense of identity may or may not imply any sort of concerted action. For example, a fan of a particular music artist may feel part of a group that shares that interest. However, it's highly unlikely that fan would be invested enough to go to war against a rival group of music fans or even engage beyond buying the artist's music and occasionally attending a concert.

Understanding levels of engagement and what groups mean to people is a key task for sociologists who are interested in understanding social organization. The topic inspires two interrelated questions: Should sociologists always focus on categories of groupness? Or should they instead focus their attention on actions? Scholars who take the latter approach often focus on **group boundaries** and the ways that people form and police distinctions between themselves and others. These **boundary processes** reveal how people think about their own identities and who is included (or not) as a member of a group.

The study of formal organizations takes a related but somewhat different approach. Organizations are often more hierarchically and formally structured than groups, which can be loosely defined. Sociologists studying formal organizations are interested in the ways people constitute these **hierarchies** and how individuals relate to each other within them.

Organizations impact people's lives in many ways and on many levels, from employers to large, society-wide structures such as state and national governments and their divisions, like the DMV or the social security office.

One of the first sociologists to study organizational processes was **Max Weber**, who was deeply interested in the types of **bureaucratic** processes that have become so important in modern states. Weber examined how organizations and institutions outlive any individual member, creating larger social structures. Other sociologists have focused on the clash between inertia and **institutional change**. Who decides what an organization or institution will do? And how do power struggles within an organization determine who is in control of policy and procedures?

Living in society, people must frequently interact with organizations but are also a part of them. And even though organizations regulate people's lives, social movements and collective action have shown that these social structures do not have total control. Social change is always occurring, and enough concerted effort can change organizations and institutions to reflect new social interests and beliefs.

CONCLUSION

As the growth and effectiveness of social movements demonstrate, society is never static but is instead always in a state of flux. Sociologists are often interested in how societies change and how the complicated interplay of social institutions, organizations, movements, and processes determine which aspects of society change and which stay the same. Sociologists focus on a wide range of social phenomena—including culture, social groups, institutions, and organizations—to understand the different processes operating in society. These processes of socialization influence the attitudes and actions of people in their daily lives and shape how and what people become and how they interact with society.

Ultimately, social processes exert social control, encouraging people to act in particular ways that a society deems palatable. When people deviate from those expectations, they face social consequences. But sometimes deviance leads to relationships with other deviant social actors and a sense that it is society itself that is out of step with how the world should be. Enough actors working together can create social movements and collective action in such a way as to force social and institutional change. By tracing these processes, sociologists gain insight into how and why a society changes and what social change is likely in the future.

READINESS CHECK: SOCIAL PROCESSES

To check how well you understand the concepts covered in this chapter, review the following questions. If you have trouble answering any of them, consider reading through this chapter again and reviewing the key terms before moving on to the next chapter.

- Why is social interaction important to the science of sociology?
- What are the differences between micro and macro patterns of social interaction? What are examples of each?
- What is culture? What are the differences between these cultural distinctions?
  - Popular culture
  - High or elite culture
  - Counterculture
  - Subculture
- What was the focus of Pierre Bourdieu's book *Distinction*?
- What are the two forms of social change?
- What are the three models of social change?
- What is socialization? What role do agents of socialization have in a person's life? What/who are some prominent socializers in a person's life?
- What is the sociological perspective of deviance? What are some examples of behaviors that would be considered deviant?
- What is the purpose of social sanctions?
- What initiates a social movement? What do activists do to frame a social issue? How do countermovements relate to social movements?
- What were the contributions of Durkheim and Weber to organizational studies?

TEST YOURSELF: SOCIAL PROCESSES

Directions: Each of the questions or incomplete statements below is followed by five suggested answers or completions. Select the one best answer for each. The Answer Key and Explanations will follow.

1. Which of the following best defines the Black Lives Matter and All Lives Matter movements?

   A. Movement and countermovement
   B. Frame and conclusion
   C. Primary socializers
   D. Anthropological cultures
   E. Countercultures

2. Social change is _____.

   A. unlikely
   B. the result of socialization processes
   C. deviant
   D. constantly happening in one form or another
   E. the sole result of elites changing society

3. Which of the following represents a social sanction against deviance?

   A. Grading a university exam on a curve
   B. Mocking someone for dressing inappropriately
   C. Protesting government policies
   D. Reposting content from a social media influencer
   E. Failing an exam in college

4. Pierre Bourdieu's theories in his book *Distinction* focus on the difference between

   A. anthropology and sociology
   B. high and low cultures
   C. popular culture and counterculture
   D. conformity and deviance
   E. taste and socialization

5. All of the following examples meet the definition of a group EXCEPT

    A. residents of an apartment complex who meet to discuss a book each month

    B. fans of a sports team who meet at a bar to watch each game

    C. people living in the same neighborhood who shop for groceries at the same store

    D. students at a school who start an advocacy group to celebrate their cultural heritage

    E. members of a political party who meet to plan potential laws to address social issues

Answer Key and Explanations

1. A	2. D	3. B	4. B	5. C

1. **The correct answer is A.** Black Lives Matter (BLM) developed as a movement opposed to police violence against the Black community while the All Lives Matter movement arose in response to the framing used by BLM. Countermovements are defined as groups who are invested in maintaining the status quo—those who are resistant to social change—which best fits the given examples.

2. **The correct answer is D.** Because of different trends, changes in technology and communication, and normal differences in attitude between older and younger generations, society is constantly in flux as different pressures and movements seek to create social change. Social change might occur in response to socialization (choice B), be considered deviant (choice C), or be initiated by certain groups (choice E), but it cannot be said that these choices are true in all cases.

3. **The correct answer is B.** Mocking someone is an effort to control behavior through informal negative sanctions—an attempt to discourage deviance and insist on accepted norms of fashion and self-presentation. Choices A, D, and E are not actions meant to discourage specific behavior, so they do not qualify as a sanction, and choice C discourages actions taken by a group that is in power, which generally implies a lack of deviance and thus does not match the criteria of a social sanction.

4. **The correct answer is B.** Pierre Bourdieu was most interested in the question of taste and what distinguished the tastes of the elite, otherwise known as high culture, from those of the working class, sometimes known as low culture.

5. **The correct answer is C.** Groups are defined as a collection of people who share a characteristic and take action to emphasize that characteristic. While living in a certain neighborhood does constitute a shared characteristic that could lead to group formation in some cases, shopping at a grocery store does not reinforce or emphasize that shared characteristic in any organized way. Thus, the people described in choice C would not qualify as a group.

Chapter 7

Social Stratification

OVERVIEW

- Social Class
- Social Mobility
- Race and Ethnic Relations
- Sex and Gender Roles
- Aging
- Professions and Occupations
- Power and Social Inequality
- Conclusion
- Readiness Check: Social Stratification
- Test Yourself: Social Stratification

Modern societies are never homogeneous—they consist of diverse groups of different people that belong to different social categories. These categories are often related to power and social status, and divisions between categories often result in unequal access to resources, such as income, opportunity, and access to services.

Sociologists call this circumstance **social stratification**, a term derived from the geological term *strata* that describes different layers of rock. Just as geologists study rock stratification, sociologists study social stratification, the system of social categorization used to differentiate people within a society. Sociologists also analyze the consequences of the resulting inequalities in various dimensions of social life and for various groups of people. Given its central role in the study of sociology, social stratification is the subject of 25% of the questions on the CLEP Introductory Sociology exam.

SOCIAL CLASS

The study of social stratification is most closely associated with the study of social or **socioeconomic** class. **Class** refers to a group of individuals sharing a particular set of economic circumstances. In the United States, discussions of class most commonly refer to the **upper class**, **middle class**, and **working** or **lower class**. Sociologists argue that people who are categorized as belonging to one of these classes share a set of economic realities and that their life experiences are shaped by their access or lack of access to financial resources. Social classes in the United States are particularly stratified, meaning the differences between them are significant and the boundaries are distinct. The wealthiest people in the United States have far more resources than the poorest, and the lives of the people in each group are radically different.

Sociologists have been studying social class since the discipline's inception. Social class was the primary concern of **Karl Marx**, one of the foundational figures of sociology. For Marx, **class struggle** was the primary driver of human history: everything that has ever happened in human society can be traced to concerns over and competition for economic resources.

Marx's theory relied on a different set of social classes than those most familiar to sociologists today. For Marx, the primary distinction in society was between those who owned the **means of production**—a term describing the resources needed to produce material goods, such as factories, machinery, and raw materials—and those whose only resource was **labor**, which could be sold to employers in exchange for enough money to live. Marx called these two groups the **bourgeoisie** and **proletariat**, respectively. He argued that the capitalist economic system relies on these social categories and is designed to advantage wealthy business owners at the expense of their workers, extracting profit from workers while offering them little in return.

More recent scholars have built on Marx's ideas by asking questions like
- What do economic classes look like today?
- Why does society have such stratified systems of social and economic life?
- What are the consequences of these types of social distinctions?
- How does socioeconomic stratification differ across different types of societies and social structures?

The types of **economic inequality** that exist in a society are a product of its economic system and the policy decisions it makes to structure its economic life. Some theories suggest that economic inequality is a good thing and that large differences between the wealthy and the poor encourage everyone to work harder. People in lower classes work to achieve the rewards available in a higher social class, while those in the upper classes work to avoid losing their advantages and resources. Societies that espouse these ideologies are likely to construct economic systems that create advantages for having wealth, including lower tax rates, incentives for investment, and limited **social welfare** spending.

Other societies prefer a system that privileges **economic equality**, believing that it is beneficial to all to raise the floor and limit the ceiling of the economic status that people can reach. Societies with this sort of **ideology** are more likely to increase tax rates and invest in social welfare spending in an attempt to limit the differences between the wealthiest and the poorest in their society.

Social class matters to sociologists because it plays a powerful role in other areas of social life. In the United States, in particular, higher economic standing provides access to advantages that are not available to people in other social strata. **Socioeconomic status** is strongly tied to health in the United States, as wealthier populations have more access to health care, to better and more nutritious foods, and to jobs and living conditions further removed from environmental pollution and unhealthy air and water. Wealth provides access to better schools, safer neighborhoods, and more stability. Moreover, because wealth tends to remain within families that have it and continues to grow, the wealthier classes have more opportunity to secure their upper-class status for future generations; sociologists refer to this as **generational wealth**.

Conversely, poverty is associated with a host of other social challenges beyond economic struggles. Poorer people face tougher working conditions, limited access to job opportunities, diminished access to social services, and other disadvantages. Sociologist **Matthew Desmond** chronicled many of these challenges in his Pulitzer Prize–winning book *Evicted*, which examined the experiences of poorer populations in Milwaukee, Wisconsin. What Desmond found was that poverty often becomes **generational poverty**: the social conditions that lead to the poverty of one generation of a family put future generations at a disadvantage. Poverty can be devastating, and social systems can make it incredibly difficult for people in lower classes to climb to a higher rung of the socioeconomic ladder.

SOCIAL MOBILITY

Social class is a powerful structural component of society that separates those with resources from those without. A fundamental ideology in the United States, however, is that such social divisions are not fixed, forever keeping people at one level of socioeconomic status. Instead, all people are said to have the opportunity to move up the proverbial ladder. This kind of movement between social classes is called **social mobility**. Sociologists measure social mobility in a variety of ways. One measure is purely **economic**, exploring increases or decreases in income levels. Other measures focus on **social status** or **types of professions**.

Sociologists can examine these dimensions either within a single lifetime or across generations. By evaluating a person's socioeconomic status at birth and at death and tracing changes in status throughout their life, sociologists can assess **intragenerational mobility**. In contrast, the differences between generations of people, assessed by comparing a person's socioeconomic status to that of their parents and grandparents, represent **intergenerational mobility**. When considering intergenerational mobility, sociologists can include characteristics beyond income level, such as occupation.

Sociologists analyzing intergenerational mobility ask questions like
- How does this person's occupation differ from the occupation(s) of their parent(s)?
- Did this person enter a profession primarily because it is what their parent(s) chose, or did they have the opportunity to strike out on their own in new ways?
- Did this person require more or less education for their profession than the generations before them needed?
- Does this person's profession bring more esteem than those of the generations before them?

These types of questions allow sociologists to explore the mobility of different types of people across socioeconomic classes over time and evaluate the influence of that mobility on societal development across long periods of time.

A fundamental sociological theory introduced by **Max Weber** to explore questions of social mobility relies on the concept of **life chances** (*Lebenschancen* in German). Life chances are the opportunities people have to improve their quality of life through access to valuable social and economic resources such as education, health care, or high-paying employment. According to Weber's theory, life chances are directly correlated to socioeconomic status and greatly affect how much social mobility a person has in their lifetime.

The United States prides itself on being a society in which anyone can make their own fortune. Enough hard work and dedication might allow someone to "pull themselves up by their bootstraps" and ascend from one social class or socioeconomic status to another. Stories abound about self-made men like Horatio Alger rising from rags to riches over the course of a single lifetime. In many cases, these stories are true; the social class system in the United States has permeable barriers, and success stories are frequently lauded in media and popular culture.

For the most part, however, social mobility is relatively rare and hard to attain. Structural barriers—stratified neighborhoods separating rich and poor, unequal access to education, and limited life chances and choices for those less privileged—make it very difficult for people to move to a higher social class. The economic mobility that does exist is more frequently negative than positive; it is far more common to lose wealth and status due to lifestyle choices, mismanagement of wealth, or simple bad luck.

Those who do achieve upward social mobility do so largely through education. **Educational attainment** is the single characteristic most closely linked to meaningful economic change in a person's life. This relationship is highlighted in studies that have shown an increase in annual income for each extra year of school completed. People who achieve certain educational milestones, such as graduating from high school, college, and graduate school, see that each opens opportunities for increased earnings over their lifetime. Education, too, can increase access to jobs that are more highly esteemed in a society. In the United States, the type of effort and knowledge accumulation presumed to come with more years of schooling and higher credentials tends to be valued highly.

The deep connections between education, life chances, and social inequality demonstrate how important education systems and opportunities can be in driving social mobility. When people of all classes have access to education and to different types of jobs and opportunities, social mobility increases. Societies that limit access to education are more likely to limit social mobility. Even in societies that offer diverse educational opportunities and welcome the contributions of people across social classes, social mobility can still be hard to achieve. Those hoping to move up the socioeconomic ladder face a certain level of systemic inertia, and they often face significant barriers even when they manage to access higher levels of education. This reality demonstrates the power of social stratification to limit social mobility.

RACE AND ETHNIC RELATIONS

Another important component of stratification and inequality in society is the relationships between different racial and ethnic groups. From its origin, the societal landscape of the United States has been a tremendously racialized one. Both race and ethnicity have had—and continue to have—a powerful impact on the life chances and life choices of people in the United States.

Even before the United States was founded, explorers and colonists from Europe came into conflict with Indigenous populations. Much of the rhetoric about these conflicts was based on racist ideas about the need to spread European civilization to the inhabitants of newly "discovered" territories. **Ethnocentric** ideas about entitlement to land supported European **colonization**, and powerful narratives about manifest destiny were based on beliefs that white Europeans and the societies they built were more civilized than any others. Indigenous people were not the only racial or ethnic group exploited in the early history of the United States: the economic system was founded on the racial exploitation and enslavement of Black people brought to the United States from countries in Africa and other parts of the world and sold to white landowners. This system of slave labor created wealth for white Americans through the exploitation of an entire racial group.

The social and economic damage that slavery wrought on generations of people is still present in social inequalities that persist today. Even after slavery was made illegal, a wide range of rules and policies systematically targeted and harmed already disadvantaged Black Americans. These included the imposition of Jim Crow laws in the South after the Civil War that segregated all public facilities, the redlining of neighborhoods that created and perpetuated housing inequality, and the targeted policing of Black populations by law enforcement. The civil rights movement, led by figures such as Martin Luther King Jr. and Rosa Parks, pushed the United States to change some of the legal inequalities in American society, codifying the protection of racial equity in pursuit of a more racially equitable society.

Though formal laws that enforced racial inequality in the United States have been abolished, patterns of social organization and social systems are harder to change. **Structural inequality**—inequality built into the system itself—persists due to inertia, regressive attitudes, and a history of disadvantage. Crucially, this means that inequalities persist even when most people today claim to want equality and deny harboring any form of racism. The impact of history is strong: people of color are still more likely to live in poorer neighborhoods than white Americans because of redlined housing laws that only designated certain neighborhoods, often the least desirable, as available to people of color. Furthermore, Black families in the United States tend to have far less generational wealth than white families due to the historical inequities encountered by generations of Black families before them.

The repercussions of structural inequality are vast. If you live in a poorer neighborhood, your home has a lower property value, which makes it more difficult to gather enough financial resources to move into a better neighborhood. Your access to health care, quality schooling, and high-paying jobs are similarly compromised, a fact of life for people of color in the United States. These types of inequalities persist for generations, despite a variety of efforts to ameliorate them. On almost every measure of economic status, Black, Latino, and Native American populations score well below white populations. Statistics such as these belie the idea of the United States as a racially equal society where social mobility is equally available to all. Historical forms of inequality have persisted into the present day, taking on different forms and working in different ways but perpetuating a society in which inequality between racial and ethnic groups is a constant and powerful part of social life.

SEX AND GENDER ROLES

Sex and **gender**, characteristics that shape many life experiences and opportunities, are also major components of stratification and inequality within society. Sex and gender are related but distinct concepts, though the terms are often confused and misused. *Sex* refers to biological distinctions—the genitalia, chromosomes, and hormones—that shape physical bodies, and people are categorized as biologically male, female, or intersex. *Gender* is a more complex distinction; it refers to personal identity and it also frequently denotes corresponding sets of social roles. Scholars within and outside of sociology now recognize that gender identity is not binary but a spectrum spanning a wide range of possible identities and gender expressions with which people may identify. Inequalities based on sex and gender may take a variety of forms.

One area of social stratification in which social inequality is prevalent is **gender roles**. Members of a given society often have a standard set of criteria for what it means to be a man or a woman and what types of behaviors, activities, appearances, and personality traits are associated with those identities. Historically, many societies have tended to ascribe gender roles based on sex, and male children have been raised to adopt the gender roles expected of men and female children to adopt the gender roles expected of women.

In the United States, men have typically been expected to be the heads of the household, responsible for financially supporting a family and performing a specific set of household duties. Women have typically been expected to be nurturers, responsible for caring for children, supporting the household, and accomplishing much of the everyday business of household labor. Gender roles typically extend to emotional and behavioral expectations as well. Stereotypical expectations are for men to be strong and distant, rarely sharing emotions other than anger, and women to be weaker, prone to excessive emotion, and more caring and nurturing. These are vast generalizations, of course, but these stereotypes create important social expectations that dictate appropriate behavior. People are socialized to act in a particular way and limited, or at least discouraged, from engaging in some types of behaviors and pursuits. Socialization of gender roles happens on a society-wide basis, meaning that each member of a society tends to internalize these norms, even if unintentionally.

The way societies across the world have gendered particular types of behaviors, attitudes, and roles is deeply unequal. Women (and many minoritized groups) are often socially sanctioned for possessing attributes or demonstrating behaviors that men (or dominant groups) are praised for demonstrating. Traits seen as indicating confidence, assertiveness, or indignance in a man might be disparaged as pushiness, bossiness, or hysteria in a woman. A man's dedication to his career is often seen as admirable, but a woman's is often judged in terms of its effect on her family.

Inequalities like these in sex and gender are visible in a range of social arenas. Sociologist **Arlie Russell Hochschild** studied the division of labor in romantic relationships and found that women do far more housework than men, contributing roughly 70% of household labor time. Men contribute 15% (and children the other 15%), but when men were surveyed, they reported that they contributed equally. Domestic and intimate partner violence also affects women at much higher rates than men, particularly because most violence is perpetrated by men. The rates of violence against **transgender** and **nonbinary** people also very high, and these groups also face mental health and social challenges at rates far exceeding those of **cisgender** populations.

There is also a significant wage gap that persists between men and women. Sociologists have attempted to determine the cause of this distinction for a long time. Some argue that it is the result of socialization. They assert that from early on, people are encouraged to follow specific career paths and develop certain interests that are considered proper for their perceived sex and gender. Other sociologists highlight the societal expectation for women to be responsible for raising children and taking care of the home and argue that women self-select out of the job market. By choosing jobs that pay less but offer more flexibility for time off or by leaving the workforce entirely during their children's early years, these women fall behind men who stay in full-time jobs. Some sociologists have also pointed to biases in employer attitudes, arguing that many employers, either consciously or subconsciously, expect men to fulfill certain roles and then hire accordingly. Regardless of its cause(s), the wage gap is yet another component of inequality inherent in the social stratification of sex and gender roles.

AGING

Aging is not always a factor people consider in terms of social stratification. Economics, race, gender, and sexuality are all more familiar arenas for discussing the topic of stratification and the inequalities faced by different categories of people in society. Yet the study of how people interact with and are viewed by society across their lifespans can be critically important to understanding certain components of social stratification. Sometimes sociologists focus on **generations**, meaning cohorts of people within a relatively well-defined age range. There are many problems with dividing people up into sharply defined categories by age, not the least being that births are largely continuous and don't conform to simplistic temporal divisions. However, the concept of generations has become a useful way to describe differences between younger and older segments of a population and common life experiences of different groups.

The distribution of a population across age ranges can make a powerful impact on the characteristics of a society—and its priorities. The United States, for example, saw a sharp increase in births immediately after the end of World War II. The resulting generation of children, called **baby boomers**, was larger than previous and later generations, and their **life course** has shaped much of American social life well into the 21st century. When this group came of working age, the United States had a large and available workforce contributing to the economy and paying into programs such as Social Security. As this population has aged, the country has had to manage a declining workforce and a sharp increase in withdrawals from those programs to fund their retirements. This has shifted the balance between working and retired populations and even created tension between baby boomers and the succeeding generations, who sometimes feel that baby boomers had better opportunities and are now benefitting unduly from the younger generations' labor. These types of intergenerational tensions can permeate many aspects of social life.

Additionally, aging often is accompanied by increasing health care needs. The United States is facing a so-called "gray wave" as the population of seniors grows. This generation of seniors is not only more numerous than generations before, but people are also living increasingly longer lives as modern medicine improves. Given the many inequalities in access to health care in the United States, the increasing needs of a large senior population have become an ever more pressing issue.

Medical advances do make it possible for people to continue working and living more active lives longer than ever before. This is good for people and the society they contribute to, but it does affect the composition of the workforce as seniors retain positions longer before retiring and making them available to younger generations. This can delay opportunities for younger members of society until much later in their lives. Sociologists have found that this delay also leads to delays in other important social markers: people get married later, have children later, and buy houses, if they are able to at all, much later in life than previous generations.

Older Americans have retained their positions in many other sectors of society as well. Politics in the United States, for example, has increasingly become the domain of the elderly. Between 2000 and 2023, the average age of the four US presidents at inauguration was 62.25 years, and the latter two presidents' average was 74 years. As of 2023, the average age of members of Congress was higher than ever before, and surveys of younger generations—**Gen X, millennials,** and **Gen Z**—reveal that these younger

Americans are increasingly disenchanted with the political system and feel like they are not represented by the candidates who have the resources and opportunity to seek office.

For all the advantages that younger generations might feel older generations have in society, aging is a unique process that has its own set of disadvantages and can also entail a slow separation from social life and opportunity. As children grow up and move away, friends and partners die, and challenges to health and mobility mount, older members of society can become vulnerable to isolation and loneliness. Sociologists increasingly find that many older populations face economic challenges as they lose their ability to work and provide for themselves or adjust to living on a fixed income.

Unlike many other characteristics by which people are categorized, aging is a process that affects everyone. Social roles and responsibilities change as children grow into adults and then again as adults age, necessitating new relationships with the society around them. How a society responds to the needs of its older generations may heavily influence the shape of that society.

PROFESSIONS AND OCCUPATIONS

Professions and occupations are another category by which social strata are defined. Occupational opportunities and experiences are inextricably tied to socioeconomic status, race and ethnicity, sex and gender, age, education, disability status, immigration status, and a whole host of other demographic dimensions. As with any category of social stratification, inequalities exist in the power, social status, and access to resources of different professional or occupational positions.

Labor is essential to the economic function of a society, and society rewards people for their professional and occupational labor and contributions to social life. These rewards are allocated based on a variety of criteria, including a person's status. **Status** is the amount of esteem a person has in society; it demonstrates the value society places on the contributions of a particular person or type of labor. Higher status is granted to people who are thought to be especially valuable to society. Some social rewards, like respect, are based on the types of jobs people are willing to take on for society—those in the military, for example, are often awarded a high level of respect because of their willingness to sacrifice their lives for the greater good of society. First responders, too, might earn this special sort of esteem. Doctors, college professors, or research scientists earn a different sort of esteem that is based on their educational achievements and perceived wisdom. This is a form of **educational capital**. People consider the contributions of highly educated individuals to be valuable to society and recognize the years of labor and education that sort of advanced training requires. These forms of status are powerful: even if a person is not working in a field related to their advanced degree or has retired from the military, their status can afford them opportunities that others may not have.

In addition to esteem and status, society often rewards those considered valuable with monetary compensation. Celebrities, investment bankers, entrepreneurs, and business leaders accrue significant financial reward for the jobs they do. These sorts of professions—entertainment, banking, technology, and business—are deemed particularly valuable in the capitalist economic system that drives the United States. Those who drive economic growth are seen as creators of value and rewarded accordingly.

Other professions and occupations in society that most would agree are exceptionally valuable do not garner the same economic rewards. Teachers, nurses, and even the military members and first responders earn a certain sort of social esteem but are not rewarded with the financial, educational, and social benefits that are available to people in other professions. There are many potential reasons for this, but some sociologists believe that historical inequalities in gender and socioeconomic class are significant factors. These scholars argue that the lower compensation in these fields represents a collective devaluing of women's labor in a society that does not reward women for their efforts and contributions at the scale it does men. The very term **pink-collar jobs** refers to many of these valuable but not well-compensated positions that lie in fields that were historically (and still are) dominated by women. Patterns of financial compensation show the truth of this as fields in which women predominate are undervalued, and fields in which women are increasingly joining the workforce tend to lose ground financially compared with those that continue to be dominated by men. The effects of pay inequality are multiplied for women of color.

Another possible driver of these sorts of inequalities are social attitudes and beliefs about work. Different types of labor are categorized in different ways. Many professions and occupations are jobs that are undertaken explicitly for monetary compensation, and values and stigma about poverty and wealth influence how they are perceived. Other types of labor are characterized as **vocations**, implying that they are activities to which people are "called" and choose regardless of the monetary compensation they provide. Vocations are sometimes seen as providing a different type of reward—they are more fulfilling or provide an opportunity to "make a difference"—that compensates for their low pay. This argument has even been used as justification for the low wages paid to teachers in the United States by claiming that teachers choose the profession because of their passion for teaching rather than a desire for financial success.

The types of rewards bestowed upon people in certain professions or occupations are of great interest to sociologists studying social stratification and inequality. At their core, social rewards—status, respect, educational capital, or financial compensation—reflect a person's or profession's value to society. Studying the ways that these sorts of compensation and social rewards differ reveals a great deal about what a society values and wants to incentivize; it also reveals structural and social biases and inequalities.

POWER AND SOCIAL INEQUALITY

Sociologists study social stratification to understand the systems of social categorization in a society, but the categorization is always related to social status and **power**. Sociologists think of power as the opportunity to get things done, to make things happen when you want them to, or to stop things you don't want to happen.

Power is embedded in the differences in social class and the systems of social stratification that structure societies. There are a variety of types of power outside of traditional power structures like government. Access to money is a form of power because it allows people to buy things they need and pay for services that help them accomplish goals. Social status and esteem are another form of power since people listen to those perceived to be in charge, important, highly educated, or in some other way worthy of high social status due to economic or social factors.

In large part, those at the upper reaches of a social system have more power. These positions of power provide further advantages and opportunities that are not available to others. But sociologists also study how this power can be deceptive and how it can change. Even though those in the upper classes tend to have more individual power, they are often far outnumbered by those in lower classes. Enough people working together, even those with limited personal power, can lead to drastic changes to the structures of power. As social movements throughout history have shown, unequal systems that disproportionately disadvantage too many people set the conditions for social revolution. The balance of social and economic structures is always subject to renegotiation and reform. How societies come to a consensus on what those systems look like is one of the major drivers of social and historical development.

CONCLUSION

Social stratification, the system of social categorization used to differentiate people within a society, is based on a variety of factors, including class, socioeconomic status, race and ethnicity, sex and gender, age, and professions and occupations. This categorization has a tremendous impact on the power structures in society and the types of opportunities available to different categories of people. These differences in opportunity are accompanied by material inequalities in available economic resources, access to education, and opportunities for socioeconomic advancement and participation in other economic activities.

READINESS CHECK: SOCIAL STRATIFICATION

To check how well you understand the concepts covered in this chapter, review the following questions. If you have trouble answering any of them, consider reading through this chapter again and reviewing the key terms before moving on to the next chapter.

- What is social stratification?
- How do sociologists define class and how does it relate to social stratification?
- What was Karl Marx's theory about class struggle?
- What is the status quo and how does it relate to systems of inequality?
- What policies are likely to be implemented in societies with systems designed to preserve economic inequality? What about in systems that strive to preserve economic equality?
- What is the significance of socioeconomic status?
- What are three measures of social mobility?
- What is the difference between intragenerational and intergenerational mobility?
- What are life chances?

- What is the significance of educational attainment to social mobility?
- What are some of the different types of prestige and status associated with jobs and professions in the United States? How do these affect a person's job options?
- How is social stratification manifested in the following areas?
    - Race and ethnic relations
    - Sex and gender roles
    - Aging
    - Professions and occupations
- What are generations? How does one's generation affect their relationship with society?
- What is power? Why can it be considered deceptive as it relates to social structures?

TEST YOURSELF: SOCIAL STRATIFICATION

Directions: Each of the questions or incomplete statements below is followed by five suggested answers or completions. Select the one best answer for each. The Answer Key and Explanations will follow.

1. Social stratification refers to the

   A. rewards that come from aging in society
   B. differences between sex and gender
   C. difference between vocation and occupation
   D. different categories of people in a society
   E. opportunity to get things done or stop things from happening

2. Which of the following is NOT a theory that sociologists have used to try to explain the pay gap between men and women in the United States?

   A. Socialization that encourages men and women to seek employment in different fields
   B. Sexism on the part of hiring managers
   C. Differences in the innate abilities of men and women
   D. Social expectations that women handle most childcare and domestic responsibilities
   E. Devaluation of women's labor contributions in the economy

3. Economic inequality is

   A. an innate characteristic causing extreme stratification in all human societies
   B. the product of social, political, and economic policies decided by each society
   C. the result of differences in the capabilities and work ethics of different people in society
   D. always associated with a person's contribution to society
   E. so absolute that people cannot move between social classes

4. Which of the following statements about race and ethnicity is accurate?

    A. They are concepts that have only recently been politicized in society.

    B. They are historical concepts that have little bearing on social life today.

    C. They cause social inequalities because of individual racists making individual decisions.

    D. They are overcompensated for today through policies such as affirmative action.

    E. They are socially structured patterns with deep historical roots that persist despite many people in society expressing a commitment to racial equality.

5. All of the following are examples of social mobility EXCEPT

    A. Juanita, whose parents are undocumented immigrants without high school diplomas, attends medical school and becomes a doctor.

    B. Ezekiel, whose parents were teachers, founds a tech company and becomes one of the wealthiest people in his hometown.

    C. Sanjay, who works in food service and attends a local university, wins a lottery jackpot worth $50 million.

    D. Vanessa, whose parents were college professors at a local university, earns her PhD and becomes a professor at the same university.

    E. Lucas, who was previously a union factory worker, is laid off from his job and struggles to find anything beyond low-wage entry-level positions.

Answer Key and Explanations

1. D	2. C	3. B	4. E	5. D

    1. The correct answer is D. Sociologists who study social stratification are interested in how society categorizes people using a variety of identifying characteristics. Social stratification can be based on a variety of identity markers, including race, gender, sexuality, age, socioeconomic status, family status, and more.

2. **The correct answer is C.** Sociologists focus much more on the social aspects of gender roles and the systems and beliefs that reinforce them. Choice C would be outside the purview of a sociologist in most cases. Additionally, the pay gap is visible in fields in which there are no innate differences between the capabilities of men and women, another reason choice C is the correct answer.

3. **The correct answer is B.** Economic inequality varies from society to society. The policies a society puts in place—and the shared beliefs or ideologies that inform those policies—can change the relationships between different social classes, increasing or decreasing levels of inequality.

4. **The correct answer is E.** Race has been a deeply important topic throughout US history that continues to structure social interactions today. Racial inequality and ethnic bias persist despite efforts to create a more racially just society. Much of this bias exists within the very structure of social institutions in the United States.

5. **The correct answer is D.** Social mobility refers to changes in a person's socioeconomic status, either throughout their own lifetime (intragenerational) or in relation to their parents and grandparents (intergenerational). Additionally, mobility can either be positive, in the case of choices A, B, and C, or negative, in the case of choice E. Choice D, in which Vanessa maintains a similar class status to her parents and does not experience significant change, is the only example that does not reflect social mobility.

Chapter 8

The Sociological Perspective

OVERVIEW
- The History of Sociology
- Sociological Research Methods
- Sociological Theory
- Conclusion
- Readiness Check: The Sociological Perspective
- Test Yourself: The Sociological Perspective

Sociologists approach the world from a particular perspective, one shaped by a long history of theoretical and methodological developments in the field. When scholars talk about "the sociological perspective," they are describing how sociologists view the world and how these views have shaped the history and development of sociology as a field of study. Questions about the sociological perspective constitute 20% of the material on the CLEP Introductory Sociology exam. The questions address the history of the field, the basic methods of sociological practice and research, and many of the important theories that drive sociological thought.

Despite sociology's reliance on ideas and philosophies that have been around since ancient times, most scholars believe that the foundation of sociology as we know it today came out of the sweeping changes that accompanied the European **Enlightenment**. New ideas of the time turned scholars' attention away from religious rationales for social behavior and toward different ways of thinking about people and society. Continued innovations built these first glimmers of sociological thought into a distinct social science.

Sociologists strive to understand how social phenomena form and transform, as well as the effects they have on people's lives. Sociologist **C. Wright Mills** wrote about the sociological perspective and encouraged his students to develop a **sociological imagination**—a mindset that looks for connections between the personal experiences of individuals and larger social issues. Mills thought sociologists had a responsibility to address social injustices and that seeing these connections was the first step in understanding the true causes of social injustices and working together to effect desired changes in the world.

THE HISTORY OF SOCIOLOGY

Sociology first became a distinct discipline in the mid-19th century with the writings of philosopher of science **Auguste Comte**, who developed a philosophical position prioritizing reason and logic called **positivism**. Comte and other positivists, following in the footsteps of the scientific revolution and Enlightenment thinkers of the 17th and 18th centuries, believed that all sociological study must be empirically tested and grounded in observable data. For Comte, the ideas that had revolutionized society—concepts such as the scientific method and the belief that scholars should look for physical laws rather than divine truths to explain the natural world—were deeply inspirational. He was convinced that if such ideas could be used to develop sciences such as physics and biology, they could equally apply to a science of society. Comte named this scientific endeavor sociology and hoped that it would be an all-encompassing science that could integrate all others into a grand science of humanity. Other early sociologists such as **Herbert Spencer** and **Harriet Martineau,** who also translated Comte's work, followed in this approach.

Though Comte was responsible for distinguishing and naming sociology as a separate science, many earlier thinkers pursued research that we now recognize as sociological in nature. As early as the 1st century, the Roman scholar **Tacitus** wrote what now would be considered an ethnography of Germanic tribes that the empire had encountered on its frontiers. Chinese historian and sociologist **Ma Tuan-Lin**, writing in the 13th century, emphasized the social dynamics driving historical development. In the 14th century, the Muslim scholar **Ibn Khaldun** wrote incisively about history, tribalism, and social cohesion. In Europe, throughout the Enlightenment and post-Enlightenment period, scholars such as **Karl Marx** and **Friedrich Engels** examined the changes in politics, society, and economic systems that accompanied the transition to the modern world, and **Mary Wollstonecraft** examined women's positions in society.

Early sociological work in the 19th and early 20th century was dominated by Europeans, with scholars in France and Germany leading the way. In France, **Émile Durkheim** became the first scholar to hold a post as a professor of sociology. While simultaneously working to define rules and methodologies more clearly for the newly formed field of sociology, Durkheim also examined social cohesion and the consequences of falling out of step with society. Scholars who followed him, including luminaries such as **Marcel Mauss, Claude Lévi-Strauss,** and **Pierre Bourdieu,** studied the structural elements of social life and culture, developing and contributing to the theory of **structural functionalism.**

In Germany, scholars building on the **historical materialism** of Karl Marx took an approach that emphasized the perpetual struggle over limited resources in society. Marx himself focused on the development of capitalism and the importance of capital and wage labor in socioeconomic structures. He theorized that there would always be a conflict between wealthier segments of society who owned the means of production and the wage laborers who provided the work that made production possible. Later Marxists—including theorists who congregated in Frankfurt, Germany, such as **Herbert Marcuse, Max Horkheimer, Theodor Adorno,** and **Walter Benjamin**—accepted Marx's conflict theory but added a cultural component. These **Frankfurt School** theorists studied the power of ideology and developed **Critical Theory,** a project analyzing the conditions necessary for social change and human emancipation from oppression.

Max Weber was responsible for a third sociological tradition that moved away from **positivism** toward **interpretivism,** a research method focused on interpreting actions and events in the context of the society in which they occur. Weber argued that power and social capital were at the core of social conflict, adding a new dimension to studies of how societies are organized. In his studies of religion, bureaucracy, and authority, Weber laid the foundation for sociology's consideration of ideas and day-to-day interactions as core components of social meaning. Weber, like Durkheim, was particularly interested in the role of religion in social life and whether the transition to modernity had led to disenchantment that had caused people to turn away from traditional ideas of religious belief and structure.

In the United States, too, sociology was becoming increasingly prominent as a discipline of study. Many early American sociological efforts relied heavily on Weber's ideas. **Talcott Parsons** translated both Weber's and Durkheim's books into English, combining various ideas from them to create a theory of **social action** that borrowed from structural functionalism and interpretivist approaches alike. Pioneering sociologist **W. E. B. Du Bois** worked closely with Weber, and the two exchanged ideas and visited each other. Du Bois was the first Black man to earn a PhD from Harvard, and modern sociologists increasingly credit him with some of the most important innovations in sociological work in the United States. Through his emphasis on community studies in *The Philadelphia Negro*—an empirical examination of Black neighborhoods in Philadelphia—Du Bois showed how ethnographic and community-level data can reveal social issues that deeply affect individual lives. In *The Souls of Black Folk*, Du Bois examined a group of people that white sociologists had ignored and introduced the philosophy of race to sociology.

Du Bois's new style of sociological inquiry was paralleled by researchers at the University of Chicago. Now known as the **Chicago School**, these sociologists used their location at the heart of one of the United States' most dynamic cities to conduct empirical studies of many of Chicago's immigrant neighborhoods. **Robert E. Park** developed a theory of race relations, **Ernest Burgess** examined the concentric nature of city design, and **Florian Znaniecki** examined the effects of immigration on Polish peasants. Though never formally part of the school, **Jane Addams** also worked in Chicago, developing a distinctly practical version of sociology that underlies much of the modern field of social work. **Jane Jacobs**, studying New York City in similar ways, also applied Weber's ideas about social capital to her analysis of how urban design affects communities.

George Herbert Mead, another member of the Chicago School, and **Herbert Blumer** used these analytical approaches to develop a new theory called **symbolic interactionism**, which focused on the ways humans use language to create a set of shared symbols and meanings. This process allows for social communication and provides the foundation for social cohesion. Also examining the meanings in social interactions, **Charles Horton Cooley** (a founding member and president of the American Sociological Association), created the concept of the **looking-glass self**, the idea that a person's sense of self is influenced by their interpretation of how others view them. Later scholars such as **Erving Goffman** built on these ideas to create a theory of **dramaturgical action** to examine how individuals present themselves to others.

Starting in the 1990s, sociology began to shift its focus to culture, and sociologists have increasingly focused on how cultural, religious, and other intangible aspects of social life play a powerful role in shaping everyday life. Perhaps the most important figure in this regard was French sociologist **Pierre Bourdieu**, whose book *Distinction* chronicled how cultural and social interests shape and are shaped by social stratification. Other scholars, such as **Jeffrey C. Alexander** and the anthropologist **Clifford Geertz**, have similarly centered cultural concerns at the core of their research.

In the 21st century, cultural concerns about globalization, digital sociology, criminal justice, and sociology of the environment have become the focus of much sociological work. This emphasis on contemporary social problems reveals one of the underlying goals of sociology: to explain and help solve many of the most pressing issues of our time. In many ways, tracing the history of sociology is an exercise in tracing the development and concerns of society itself. From studying the rise of modernity and decline of religion to questions of global commerce, internet communities, and mankind's role in creating and surviving environmental degradation, sociologists are always at the front lines of analyzing and exploring social change.

SOCIOLOGICAL RESEARCH METHODS

Sociologists have always been interested in establishing effective ways to study and understand the social world. Sociologists recognized that, unlike in fields such as philosophy, they would need to base their theories and arguments on empirical data. This realization led them to explore questions about which techniques and methods to use to gather necessary data, what kinds of information to analyze to help further understanding, how to verify that data represents the social world as it actually functions, and how to determine **causality** when studying the causes of social phenomena (i.e., how to determine whether one observed phenomenon is really the root cause of another).

To help with these tasks, sociologists have developed an array of **research methods**—standardized rules and procedures that help ensure they have gathered accurate data and that the conclusions drawn from their evidence are rooted in empirical reality. In general, sociological research methods can be broken down into two categories:

1. **Quantitative research methods** are practices that rely on statistical analysis of a large number of observations to determine trends.
2. **Qualitative research methods** are analyses that focus on a few cases studied in depth to discover details about the attitudes, beliefs, and experiences of research subjects.

SOCIOLOGICAL RESEARCH METHODS

Quantitative	Qualitative
Uses statistical analysis of large datasets to evaluate relationships between different variables	Uses in-depth analysis of a few cases to study complex details about research subjects
Often relies on a type of deductive reasoning	Often relies on a type of inductive reasoning
Focuses on observations of large sample sizes from which trends can be drawn	Focuses on information that is not easily quantifiable
Examples: • National or social surveys • Statistical analysis • Random sampling and oversampling • Quantitative content analysis	Examples: • Ethnography • Interviews • Historical analysis • Qualitative content analysis

Both methods can be effective, but each one is better suited to answering specific types of questions and requires a different analytical process. Sociologists must keep these differences in mind when they select their research method.

Quantitative Research

Quantitative researchers are interested in numbers; they use large datasets that allow them to evaluate the relationships between different variables. Quantitative techniques often rely on a type of **deductive reasoning**. Sociologists begin with a theory about a social phenomenon and develop a testable **hypothesis**—an educated guess about what is happening. Their research consists of the collection and analysis of data that is used to test the hypothesis to determine if it holds up to observable reality (the data collected).

As in most quantitative research, the design of an experiment involves the inclusion of one or more conditions that the researcher controls, called **independent variables**. Researchers aim to draw conclusions about how these independent variables influence a measurable outcome, called the **dependent variable**. For example, a sociologist might design a study to examine the relationship between childhood poverty and academic performance using standardized exam scores as a measure of performance. In this case, the independent variable would be family income level and the dependent variable would be academic performance. Comparing the average exam scores of children with varying family income levels would allow a sociologist to draw conclusions about the influence of childhood poverty on the academic performance of children.

When sociologists using quantitative research methods find **correlations**, meaning instances when the changes in two variables seem related to each other—students from higher-income households also having higher standardized test scores, for example—they try to determine whether those changes are connected or just a coincidence. Researchers want to know if changes noted in the dependent variable were *caused* by their relationship to the independent variable. They use a variety of **statistical tests**, including t-tests and chi-square tests, as well as more complex calculations such as logarithmic and multivariate regressions. Many of these statistical techniques are designed to search for a **statistically significant** relationship, which is a relationship that is very unlikely to have happened by chance. Statistical significance is set at the less than 0.05, 0.01, and 0.001 levels, which means that a 5% incidence or lower of a coincidence is enough for sociologists to argue that there is a distinct relationship between two variables.

Quantitative sociologists gather data in a variety of ways. Some researchers rely on large-scale national **surveys** conducted by survey companies or the US government, such as the US Census Bureau and the General Social Survey (GSS). Other researchers develop and conduct their own surveys, asking the questions most pertinent to their own specific research projects.

Designing and conducting a social survey is a complex task. Typically, researchers want a large **sample size** since statistical clarity increases as the number of respondents increases. They also want a **representative sample** of the population they are surveying. Sometimes this is accomplished with **random sampling**, in which any member of a given population is equally likely to be selected for the survey. Other times, special care is taken to ensure that every important group is well represented; this is called **oversampling**, and it can correct potential imbalances in survey responses.

Other sources of data are also suitable for quantitative analysis. Increasingly, sociologists are turning to **big data**, a term that refers to the vast amount of information collected by internet companies, social media sites, and other sources about human behavior both on the web and off. **Quantitative content analysis** is the statistical analysis of a body of written material, whether it be a newspaper, novel, blog, or any other type of written media. Researchers and computer programs can code this material and draw conclusions from detected patterns related to language use, frequency of terms and ideas, and other characteristics.

Qualitative Research

Qualitative research techniques eschew the large datasets used by quantitative researchers in favor of deeper analysis of a fewer number of cases. Qualitative research can also rely on different types of analytical reasoning but tends to rely on an **inductive** or **inverse-deductive** approach grounded in observations. Instead of starting with a theory and empirically testing hypotheses like deductive reasoning, inductive reasoning begins with a set of empirical observations and seeks to identify patterns within that data from which to build theories. Data used for qualitative research can take many different forms, but a unifying characteristic of qualitative research is a focus on information that is not easily quantifiable. Important qualitative research techniques include documenting ethnographic observations, conducting interviews, analyzing historical documents, and performing qualitative content and thematic analysis.

Ethnography entails a sustained, in-depth observation of a community or culture. Ethnographers embed themselves in the social settings they study, engaging in participant observation. They may take on roles at the outskirts of the social scenes they are investigating, but they sometimes become major players in the social scenes they study. Ethnographers gather data in the form of **field notes**, which are detailed sets of observations describing the social scene from the ethnographer's perspective. This is an **etic** perspective, meaning it is the perspective of an outsider looking in, as opposed to an **emic** perspective, which is the perspective of an insider. Even though they are embedded in the social scenes they analyze, ethnographers adopt an etic perspective that allows them to analyze and contextualize social and cultural phenomena.

Conducting **interviews**, in contrast, allows a researcher to document an emic understanding of social phenomena. Interviewers seek to understand a research subject's thoughts and beliefs, and the interview format allows researchers to follow up and ask deeper questions than those that can be asked in a survey. Sociologists typically conduct semistructured interviews; an interviewer prepares a general list of subjects and questions but allows the interviewee to discuss their thoughts about other relevant subjects that the interviewer may not have anticipated.

Historical analysis is the study of social change over time. Sociologists using historical analysis methods often turn to written documents—such as government documents, memoirs, letters, and newspapers—that can shed light on the social conditions in the past. Historical sociologists use these resources to explore differences across time periods, so historical analysis is often explicitly or implicitly comparative in nature. A historical sociologist might trace the development of similar structures or processes in two different societies, examining the ways societies evolve, or they might study the same society at different points in time, looking at how social change has impacted social conditions over time.

Qualitative content analysis, like its quantitative counterpart, examines a body of written material. Rather than quantifying bits of language, however, qualitative analyses seek to derive meaning by analyzing themes. These sorts of sociological research projects look for larger commonalities, ideas, and themes that appear regularly in written language and attempt to ascertain what the prevalence of these themes means about the interests and priorities of the society that created them.

Other Research Methods

Other forms of sociological analysis that don't fit squarely into either category—quantitative or qualitative—are becoming increasingly common. **Mixed methods analysis** combines the strengths of each method by using in-depth qualitative analysis to elucidate and dig deeper into trends identified in quantitative approaches. **Social network analysis** traces relationships between members of society, exploring how social life forms a web of nodes and connections and seeking to understand how those connections shape the ways people interact. Conversation analysis works on a granular level by exploring how word choice, body language, and other forms of communication shape personal interactions in society.

This wide variety of research techniques highlights the diversity of sociology as a discipline and the tremendous array of social phenomena and questions researchers are exploring. Each of these methods is best suited to a particular type of inquiry and each has strengths and weaknesses. Sociologists choose between them based on which one is best suited to answer the types of questions they want to ask. Each method provides a systematic, organized way for sociologists to study the development, structure, and function of society.

SOCIOLOGICAL THEORY

Sociological theory provides a lens through which sociologists can view and interpret the world. Larger theoretical concepts and perspectives offer a framework for understanding social systems and guide sociological inquiry. As social scientists, sociologists are interested in identifying the rules and norms that govern social behavior, and social theories play a powerful role in the discovery process. These broad theories about society are informed by social phenomena, historical events, and systems of power that exist in different societies. Sociologists often use the theories of other social scientists and philosophers to create new theories and schools of thought. New areas of sociological inquiry and scholarship continue to interact with and inform sociologists' understanding of the major theories that have defined the discipline of sociology: conflict theory, structural functionalism, and symbolic interactionism.

MAJOR SOCIOLOGICAL THEORIES

Theory	Description	Principal Theorists
Conflict theory	Theory that society is in constant conflict due to unequal distribution of resources; scarcity results in different groups attempting to retain or acquire resources	• Karl Marx • Max Weber • Ralf Dahrendorf
Structural functionalism	Theory that the structure of society relies on different interdependent members and institutions that must work together to function and achieve social stability	• Émile Durkheim • Herbert Spencer • Robert Merton • Talcott Parsons
Symbolic interactionism	Microtheory that individual interactions between people in their daily lives determine how meaning is conveyed and that these relationships shape individual behaviors	• George Herbert Mead • Herbert Blumer • Charles Horton Cooley

Though sociological work has diversified and branched out significantly since its early days, most sociologists still work within one of the three major traditions that were established early in the discipline's history. These theories offer different perspectives on the topics all sociologists must grapple with in their study of society. The following sections outline each of these traditions of sociological theory and how they are used by sociologists.

Conflict Theory

Conflict theory is based on the theory of Karl Marx and other theorists interested in understanding the power dynamics of modern society. For conflict theorists, the distribution of resources in a society determines its power and social structures, and a scarcity of resources means that different sectors of society will always be in conflict, trying either to retain or acquire resources.

Marx believed that this conflict was always associated with social class. The first chapter of *The Communist Manifesto*, the famous book by Marx and Friedrich Engels, begins with the striking declaration that "the history of all hitherto existing society is the history of class struggle." Marx and Engels describe the driving force behind all social dynamics in a capitalist society as the struggle between the dominant **bourgeoisie** (those who own the means of production) and the working-class proletariat (those who provide the labor necessary for production).

Other theorists have used Marx's theory but added nuance or applied the framework to other social structures. Max Weber emphasized the importance of social class but also argued that other forms of capital, such as status and party affiliation, played a role in **social stratification** and social conflict. He asserted that many types of power rely on different dimensions of social strat-ification to structure society, generally operating in a way that ensures that those who have power will maintain it. Sociologists studying race and gender often use the theoretical framework of conflict theory to argue that racial and gender inequalities arise from the dominance of white men and that the sys-tems of power that privilege this group operate at the expense of other groups.

Structural Functionalism

Structural functionalism, in contrast to conflict theory, focuses on pro-cesses of social cohesion and the ways different members and institutions in society work together to help society function. Structural functionalists offer theories about why and how complex structures of social life form and persist and why members of societies agree to a wide variety of conditions that constrain their own individual freedoms in service of social order.

Structural functionalists believe that being social and building social structures is fundamental human behavior but that the structures of soci-eties depend on a variety of social conditions. Émile Durkheim, the most influential sociologist in this theoretical tradition, argued that the division of labor in a society was deeply important to its social functioning. In premodern societies, he argued, there was little differentiation in how labor was assigned: in small villages, for example, every person did the same tasks, planting crops, harvesting them, and producing other types of resources. People felt connected through their similarities in a socially cohesive and integrated society, a situation that Durkheim called **mechanical solidarity**.

Most societies today function very differently, with people specializing in different tasks. Farmers grow food, factory workers produce manufactured goods, and professors write sociology books, but they all do so in a way that contributes to society as whole. Durkheim called this situation, in which people contribute to society according to their own unique positions, **organic solidarity**.

Structural functionalists argue that the social organization created by a system with organic solidarity is so powerful that social structures, institutions, and professions persist only as long as they serve a function— those that are no longer useful will not survive. As a result, if something does still exist in society, it must be serving some important social role, even if not an obvious one. For structural-functionalist sociologists, studying the social structures in a society is a major component of determining how that society functions.

Symbolic Interactionism

Symbolic interactionism is a theory concerned with social phenomena on a smaller scale. Rather than theorizing about the large-scale organization of societies, symbolic interactionists study individual interactions between people in their daily lives, seeking to understand how meaning is conveyed and how relationships shape individual behaviors. Symbolic interactionists such as Herbert Blumer and George Herbert Mead studied the symbols, ideas, and beliefs conveyed in everyday conversations. Charles Horton Cooley argued that these types of interactions shape each person's self-understanding, a concept he called the looking-glass self to describe how people rely on their perceptions of how others perceive them to form their self-concepts.

An important component of symbolic interactionism is interpretation. A person always interprets their interactions with others and the actions of others based on their personal perspective and assessment, but they also operate within and are influenced by a system of shared meanings. Any time a person immediately knows (or wonders) how to act in a social situation, they are relying on their understanding (or lack of understanding) of collective interpretations of shared meanings. Sociologists operating with a symbolic interactionist perspective believe that everyday situations and interactions are powerful indicators of the systems of shared understanding that form the foundation of all social life.

CONCLUSION

Sociologists frame their study of society using a perspective based in sociological theory, relying on the rich history of sociology, and using sociological research methods that were developed to provide insight and data about the questions they seek to answer. These traditions are the product of centuries of sociological work, as generations of social theorists, philosophers, and researchers have worked to further their understanding of the social world. The sociological perspective is informed by this rich history that continues to influence how sociologists understand and study society today.

READINESS CHECK: THE SOCIOLOGICAL PERSPECTIVE

To check how well you understand the concepts covered in this chapter, review the following questions. If you have trouble answering any of them, consider reading through this chapter again and reviewing the key terms before moving on to the next chapter.

- What are the two main sociological research methods and how do they differ? What would be good examples of each? How would they be used in different scenarios?
- What are the three main sociological theories? How are they defined? Which might apply to certain scenarios?
- Who were these thinkers and what primary theories or work did they contribute to sociology?
  - Jane Addams
  - Herbert Blumer
  - Pierre Bourdieu
  - Auguste Comte
  - W. E. B. Du Bois
  - Émile Durkheim
  - George Herbert Mead
  - Charles Horton Cooley
  - Karl Marx
  - Talcott Parsons
  - Max Weber
  - Mary Wollstonecraft

TEST YOURSELF: THE SOCIOLOGICAL PERSPECTIVE

Directions: Each of the questions or incomplete statements below is followed by five suggested answers or completions. Select the one best answer for each. The Answer Key and Explanations will follow.

---

1. A scholar who develops a theory and then tests it using empirical research is likely using

   A. deductive reasoning
   B. inductive reasoning
   C. ethnographic methods
   D. symbolic interaction
   E. conversation analysis

2. The idea that social inequalities between genders are the result of status advantages granted to men at the expense of women is a perspective likely rooted in which sociological theory?

   A. Structural functionalism
   B. Organic solidarity
   C. Symbolic interactionism
   D. Multivariate regression
   E. Conflict theory

3. Which of the following is regarded as one of the first feminist theorists due to their writing about the status of women in society?

   A. Karl Marx
   B. Mary Wollstonecraft
   C. Jane Addams
   D. Max Weber
   E. Harriet Martineau

4. A sociologist who decided to study a particular subculture by attending events for and participating in social structures of that culture while taking notes on their observations is engaged in

A. quantitative content analysis
B. social network analysis
C. ethnographic analysis
D. historical analysis
E. big data analysis

5. Which of the following would interest a sociologist studying the looking-glass self?

A. The correlation between union membership and wage stagnation in the 20th century
B. The differences between how students speak to teachers and how they speak to other students
C. The impact of religion on moral beliefs and attitudes about deviance
D. The experiences of people who withdraw from social roles as they age
E. The contrasting historical images of civil rights leaders like Malcolm X and Martin Luther King Jr. presented by public schools

Answer Key and Explanations

1. A	2. E	3. B	4. C	5. B

1. **The correct answer is A.** Deductive reasoning is often used for quantitative work and involves researchers starting with a theoretical proposition and testing that proposition by gathering data. Inductive reasoning (choice B) begins with a set of empirical observations and seeks to identify patterns within that data from which to build theories. Ethnographic methods (choice C) are hands-on methods like a sociologist embedding themselves in a social scene, making detailed observations, and participating in the social phenomena they study. Symbolic interactionism (choice D) is a social theory unrelated to experiment methodology. Conversation analysis (choice E) is a research technique that explores how word choice, body language, and other forms of communication shape interactions on the individual level.

2. **The correct answer is E.** Conflict theorists argue that resources and advantages are distributed unequally through society and conflict is inevitable as different groups seek to maximize their advantages at the expense of others. While this theory, which is rooted in the work of Karl Marx, was originally concerned with economic class, it provided the framework for future theorists to evaluate the inequalities in society that exist based on other differences, including sex and gender. Choices A, B, and C are other theoretical frameworks with less direct applications to the situation presented in this question, and choice D is a statistical technique used in quantitative research.

3. **The correct answer is B.** Mary Wollstonecraft wrote about the status of women in England and was a fierce advocate of women's rights. Neither Karl Marx (choice A) nor Max Weber (choice D) are notable for their ideas about sex and gender. While Jane Addams (choice C) was a strong advocate for women's rights, she cannot be described as one of the first feminist theorists since her work reached prominence more than a century after Mary Wollstonecraft's. Harriet Martineau (choice E) was most notable as an abolitionist and for her translations of Auguste Comte's work into English.

4. **The correct answer is C.** Ethnographic analysts embed themselves in a social scene, making detailed observations and participating in the social phenomena they study. The other choices involve analysts studying existing artifacts—such as the presence of different words, themes, or concepts within various pieces of media (choice A), interactions on social media (choice B), written materials that span different historic time periods (choice D), or the vast amounts of information gathered by internet companies that illustrate human behavior both online and offline (choice E)—rather than participating directly.

5. **The correct answer is B.** Charles Horton Cooley was famous for his concept of the looking-glass self, which posits that an individual's sense of self is developed through interpersonal interactions and management of the way they are perceived by others. Choice B relates most closely to this concept, as students speak differently within different school settings to manage how they are perceived by others, either the other students in the cafeteria or the teacher within the classroom.

Chapter 9

Practice Test

OVERVIEW

- Practice Test
- Answer Key and Explanations

An answer sheet for this test can be found on page 153.

PRACTICE TEST

This practice test and the time allotted are half the length of a full CLEP Introductory Sociology exam.

50 Questions—45 Minutes

Directions: Each of the questions or incomplete statements below is followed by five suggested answers or completions. Select the one best answer for each. The Answer Key and Explanations will follow.

---

1. Devontae was raised in a strict Christian family. He attended religious services every week, abided by the rules outlined in the Bible, and interacted primarily with other members of the church. After high school, Devontae attends a nonreligious university with a student body that has a more diverse set of religious beliefs, including atheism. Devontae decides to stop attending church because none of his friends will accompany him, and he eventually stops practicing his religion altogether. Devontae's experience is an example of a larger societal phenomenon known as

   A. secularization
   B. dogmatism
   C. modernization
   D. pluralism
   E. communism

2. What concept refers to the decentralization and expansion of urban areas into surrounding regions, often resulting in increased suburban development?

   A. Urban revitalization
   B. Urban sprawl
   C. Urbanization
   D. Gentrification
   E. Suburbanization

3. Troy uses African American Vernacular English (AAVE) when he is hanging out with his friends and Standard English when he is at work. This is an example of

A. culture shock

B. code mixing

C. code switching

D. linguistic interference

E. lexical ambiguity

4. At a concert, attendees feel a strong sense of togetherness, excitement, and shared experience. This is an example of

A. anomie

B. collective effervescence

C. positive deviance

D. subculture

E. enhanced individualism

5. When men work in jobs that are disproportionately held by women and are promoted more quickly than their female colleagues, it is called a

A. glass ceiling

B. glass escalator

C. double bind

D. layered glass ceiling

E. gender-blind hiring practice

6. Which of the following are demographic variables that demographers use to predict future populations?

I. Fertility

II. Fecundity

III. Mortality

IV. Migration

A. I and II only

B. I and III only

C. I, II, and III

D. I, III, and IV

E. II, III, and IV

7. Following the COVID-19 pandemic, Anika moves out of the city to a smaller town with lower prices, cheaper housing, and less population density while keeping her job in technology, which she now performs remotely. Her move is an example of which of the following processes?

A. Rural rebound
B. Rural revival
C. Gentrification
D. Urbanization
E. Deindustrialization

8. Which economic system is characterized by private ownership of the means of production, competition in the marketplace, and the pursuit of profit?

A. Capitalism
B. Socialism
C. Communism
D. Feudalism
E. Mercantilism

9. Which of the following terms describes a neighborhood where residents must travel several miles to reach the nearest grocery store, public transportation options are limited, and most of the available food options in the area consist of fast-food restaurants and convenience stores?

A. A food desert
B. Urban sprawl
C. Urbanization
D. A food disparity
E. Absolute poverty

10. How did the Industrial Revolution affect the physical layout of urban areas?

A. It led to the consolidation of small towns into fewer, larger cities.
B. It had no impact on the physical layout of urban areas.
C. It resulted in a decrease in population density within cities.
D. It encouraged the decentralization of cities into smaller communities.
E. It prompted the expansion of urban sprawl.

11. An organized group of people with the common aim of meeting a social goal is known as a

   A. cause
   B. social category
   C. social movement
   D. primary group
   E. secondary group

12. What term is used to describe the process of moving from one social class to another, either upward or downward, often based on changes in income or education?

   A. Socialization
   B. Social stratification
   C. Class consciousness
   D. Social mobility
   E. Social integration

13. Which type of marriage would NOT be allowed in a caste system?

   A. Endogamy
   B. Arranged marriage
   C. Exogamy
   D. Monogamy
   E. Polyandry

14. Which of the following theorists is most associated with conflict theory?

   A. W. E. B. Du Bois
   B. Émile Durkheim
   C. Robert Merton
   D. Jane Addams
   E. Karl Marx

15. Which of the following could be considered a part of the "second shift"?

A. A working mother taking on extra hours at her job to increase productivity

B. A working father getting a second job so his partner can stay at home with their child

C. A stay-at-home mother monetizing her hobby by selling art online

D. A working mother helping her child with homework each night

E. A father taking extended paternity leave so his partner can return to work

16. Which of the following is NOT a characteristic of bureaucracy?

A. Hierarchical structure

B. Formalized rules and procedures

C. Impersonal relationships

D. Decentralized decision making

E. Specialization of tasks

17. A sociologist who practices conflict theory would most likely disagree with which of the following statements?

A. Even supposedly objective measures of student ability, like SAT or other standardized test scores, offer systemic advantages to students with more wealth and cultural capital than their peers.

B. Existing social systems are reinforced by traditional power structures between students and teachers through which students learn to be agreeable and compliant to authority figures within a professional setting.

C. Public schools serve several latent functions, such as providing opportunities for courtship and the expansion of social networks, that prepare students to conform to political and social systems.

D. Tracking students based on higher or lower academic achievement creates a self-fulfilling prophecy in which students match the expectations of their teachers, and ultimately of society, reaffirming existing class divides.

E. The differences in school funding between schools in higher or lower areas of socioeconomic status condition students from working-class backgrounds to accept and retain their positions as lower-class members of society.

18. What is the primary motivation behind a countercultural movement?

    A. To conform to societal norms
    B. To create a sense of belonging within the mainstream culture
    C. To challenge and change dominant cultural values and practices
    D. To avoid cultural expression
    E. To coexist with and incorporate aspects of the dominant culture

19. Women disproportionately work in jobs that

    A. require more emotional labor
    B. pay a family wage
    C. provide education
    D. require advanced degrees
    E. encourage product creation

20. Tia owns a business and insists that anyone who interviews for the administrative assistant job have a bachelor's and master's degree. This is an example of

    A. social capital
    B. credentialism
    C. cultural capital
    D. job discrimination
    E. skill-based hiring

21. When considering the status inconsistency experienced by nurses, who have a positive social image but earn relatively little pay compared with other health care professionals, a sociologist adhering to feminist theory would likely cite

    A. historical changes in the manifest and latent functions served by medical institutions
    B. implicit gender norms that are reinforced through the hidden curriculum
    C. the historical association of the profession with women
    D. women's increased access to postsecondary education
    E. greater income stratification caused by a shrinking middle class

22. Which of the following is NOT a factor in the prestige given to occupations?

A. Compensation

B. Educational requirements

C. Level of abstract thinking required

D. Degree of autonomy

E. Diversity within the occupation

23. W. E. B. Du Bois's theory of double consciousness was meant to address

A. the need for African Americans to use two behavioral scripts to maintain their connection to Black culture while also operating in a world dominated by white culture

B. the idea that conflict between two people is the force of social change

C. the belief that sociologists need to understand the perspective of the people they study

D. the sense of a lack of consistent norms in society

E. the tension between macrosociology and microsociology

24. A religion that is characterized by alignment with a government in order to shape society, a lack of recruitment of new members because all citizens are automatically members of the religion, and highly formal religious services and practices is called a(n)

A. denomination

B. sect

C. church

D. ecclesia

E. cult

25. Émile Durkheim's theory of organic solidarity was meant to explain

   A. the rise of societies that function together despite differences in labor, values, and interests
   B. the continued prominence of religion in the postindustrialized world
   C. the importance of a system of laws and consequences to enforce social norms
   D. the growing separation between the working class and the products of their labor
   E. the tight knit social bonds that exist in societies with relatively low population density

26. A country has experienced rapid population growth over the past few decades, resulting in high population density in urban areas. Which of the following consequences is most likely to arise?

   A. Increased availability of jobs in rural areas
   B. Increased availability of jobs in urban areas
   C. Greater pressure on housing and infrastructure in cities
   D. Distrust of medical professionals
   E. Improved access to natural resources

27. Which of the following refers to the process through which individuals are taught the values, norms, and customs of their culture or society?

   A. Assimilation
   B. Cultural relativism
   C. Socialization
   D. Xenocentrism
   E. Ethnocentrism

28. A sociologist would most likely identify taking food without paying from an abandoned grocery store in the aftermath of a natural disaster as an example of

   A. conflict theory
   B. stratification
   C. altruism
   D. assimilation
   E. anomie

29. Which of the following is an example of structural mobility?

A. A high school dropout starts a multimillion-dollar company.
B. A college graduate loses their job due to a recession and takes a lower paying position.
C. A historically marginalized group gains access to education and enters higher-paid professions.
D. A skilled athlete signs a lucrative professional sports contract.
E. A factory worker earns a promotion to a managerial position.

30. All of the following social practices are associated with symbolic interactionism EXCEPT

A. sending a winking emoji to initiate a flirtatious conversation via text message
B. standing for the national anthem at a sporting event to demonstrate patriotism
C. purchasing certain products, such as clothing, to communicate social status
D. posting on social media about important social causes to appear well informed
E. driving below the speed limit to avoid receiving an expensive ticket

31. Eric is completing an ethnography tying the cooking habits of different families to their cultural customs. In addition to a survey, Eric schedules interviews with several different families to get more insight into their cultural relationships to food and cooking. Eric's choice aligns with Weber's concept of

A. anomie
B. *Verstehen*
C. *Gesellschaft*
D. *Gemeinschaft*
E. socialization

32. Who is known for his work on the concept of the sociological imagination, which encourages individuals to connect their personal experiences to larger social issues?

A. Max Weber
B. Émile Durkheim
C. Herbert Spencer
D. C. Wright Mills
E. Karl Marx

33. Ernesto is diagnosed with a serious medical condition that will require a long period of treatment. As a result, he takes an extended leave from work and disengages from many of his less serious social relationships, citing a need to rest and take care of himself as he navigates his diagnosis. Ernesto is demonstrating behavior that is typically associated with

A. the sick role
B. medicalization
C. defensive medicine
D. health care stigma
E. the patient role

34. What term is used to describe social privileges, prestigious family connections, and inherited wealth that contribute to a person's social standing?

A. Social mobility
B. Social status
C. Social class
D. Social justice
E. Social capital

35. Which of the following theories would be important to a sociologist studying microsociology?

A. Functionalism
B. Conflict theory
C. Symbolic interactionism
D. Midrange theory
E. Marxist theory

36. A group of workers at a factory engage in a labor strike to demand higher wages and better working conditions from management, who the workers believe to be overpaid. Which sociological perspective aligns with the belief of the striking workers?

A. Symbolic interactionism
B. Structural functionalism
C. Conflict theory
D. Postmodernism
E. Feminist theory

37. In the past, menopause was considered a normal biological transition in a woman's life. More recently, menopause has begun to be seen as a condition that may require medical intervention such as hormone replacement therapy. This is an example of

A. stigmatization
B. sick role
C. medicalization
D. defensive medicine
E. health care stigma

38. In the context of economic inequality, which term describes the trend where the rich become richer while the poor become poorer, leading to an increasingly large wealth gap?

A. Income mobility
B. Income stagnation
C. Income polarization
D. Income stratification
E. Income leveling

39. According to Émile Durkheim, deviance is

A. functional, normal, and universally present
B. disturbing, functional, and disruptive
C. disruptive, normal, and infrequent
D. unwarranted, frequent, and universally present
E. infrequent, unwarranted, and functional

40. Which of the following is NOT considered an example of resocialization?

A. Travis, who is 24, joins the military and goes to boot camp.
B. Destiny, who is 18 and grew up in California, moves to Canada to go to college and lives on campus.
C. Katie, who is 45, moves from Australia to Sweden to pursue her career.
D. Takeshi, who is 30, converts from Christianity to Judaism when he marries his partner.
E. Mark, who is 37, lives in the same neighborhood as his childhood home.

41. Which of the following concepts describes something that would be helpful to someone seeking new employment opportunities?

A. The strength of weak ties
B. The strength of strong ties
C. Activism
D. Positive deviance
E. Multiple dyads

42. A conflict theorist's view on stratification could best be summarized by saying that conflict arises from

A. merit-based competition
B. exploitation of one group by another group
C. governmental policies
D. deviance
E. policies that promote equality

43. Which of the following is NOT a form of stratification?

A. Caste system
B. Class system
C. Estate system
D. Status hierarchy system
E. Secret society system

44. Inga is conducting an experiment to determine the effect of stimulants on class participation in college students. She gives half of her subjects a caffeinated beverage and does not give the other half a beverage. The half of the subjects that do NOT get the beverage are the

A. study population
B. dependent variable
C. independent variable
D. control group
E. experimental group

45. Which sociologist believed that religion is the most impactful institution on social change?

A. W. E. B. Du Bois
B. Jane Addams
C. Max Weber
D. Mary Wollstonecraft
E. Auguste Comte

46. What is the primary function of a reference group for an individual?

A. To provide financial support
B. To offer emotional support
C. To serve as a benchmark for comparison and identity
D. To create a sense of exclusivity
E. To help shape political and social beliefs

47. Social control helps societies maintain

A. social order
B. social sanctions
C. activism
D. collective effervescence
E. subcultures

48. Alicia went on a date with her best friend's ex-boyfriend. Now, her friend group is not speaking to her and has not invited her to hang out with them in weeks. What kind of sanctions is Alicia facing?

A. Formal negative sanctions
B. Formal positive sanctions
C. Informal negative sanctions
D. Informal positive sanctions
E. Legal sanctions

49. Cynthia is performing an observational study in which she uses a visible security camera to assess whether age is an indicator of increased compliance with a company's handwashing policy. Since the camera is visible, Cynthia should look for ways to control for

A. nonreactive research
B. the Hawthorne effect
C. dependent variables
D. participant observation
E. meta-analysis

50. Which sociologist cofounded the American Civil Liberties Union, cofounded Hull-House, and received the Nobel Peace Prize?

A. George Herbert Mead
B. Herbert Blumer
C. Mary Wollstonecraft
D. Harriet Martineau
E. Jane Addams

ANSWER KEY AND EXPLANATIONS

1. A	11. C	21. C	31. B	41. A
2. B	12. D	22. E	32. D	42. B
3. C	13. C	23. A	33. A	43. E
4. B	14. E	24. D	34. E	44. D
5. B	15. D	25. A	35. C	45. C
6. D	16. D	26. C	36. C	46. C
7. A	17. C	27. C	37. C	47. A
8. A	18. C	28. E	38. C	48. C
9. A	19. A	29. C	39. A	49. B
10. A	20. B	30. E	40. E	50. E

1. **The correct answer is A.** Secularization denotes a societal transition away from religion, usually spurred by a lessening of the direct influence of religion on daily life. Devontae's situation, in which he moves away from his religion when it is no longer socially reinforced by his surroundings, mirrors this larger social phenomenon.

2. **The correct answer is B.** Urban sprawl is the expansion of urban areas into the surrounding regions that leads to the growth of suburbs. Choices A and D are processes that change the character of existing urban areas, and choices C and E describe population movements between urban or suburban areas of a city, neither of which necessarily require expansion.

3. **The correct answer is C.** Troy is code switching by using different varieties of the English language at work and with his friends. He would be code mixing (choice B) if he was integrating both types of English at the same time. The other choices do not apply to this scenario even though they are related to culture or linguistics.

4. **The correct answer is B.** Collective effervescence is an intensification of emotion that includes a strong sense of togetherness and harmony occurring among people in a group who participate in collective activities.

5. The correct answer is B. The term *glass escalator* refers to the phenomenon in which men are promoted more quickly than women in female-dominated professions. This is contrasted with a *glass ceiling*, which refers to the difficulty women experience in securing promotions to upper-level jobs because of internalized sexism and inequities in gender dynamics in the workplace.

6. The correct answer is D. In demography, fecundity represents the reproductive potential of a recorded population or the capacity to produce offspring, based on variables such as age. While this measure is related to population, it is not effective for population prediction. Fertility (average births), mortality (predicted deaths), and migration (population change between places) are all directly related to the prediction of future populations.

7. The correct answer is A. Rural rebound refers to the increase in population in rural counties due to people moving away from cities and suburbs. Choices B and C relate to economic investment in an existing area, which is not reflected in Anika's situation, and choices D and E do not apply to population movement from urban to rural areas.

8. The correct answer is A. Capitalism stresses the importance of private ownership to incentivize market efficiency and maximize profits, in contrast with choices B and C, and it also values competition between different economic entities to drive innovation, distinguishing it from choices D and E.

9. The correct answer is A. While the other choices may also apply to a neighborhood like the one described, the specific details about inaccessible grocery stores and limited food options outside of fast-food restaurants and convenience stores indicate that this neighborhood would be defined by sociologists as a food desert.

10. The correct answer is A. During the Industrial Revolution, many people moved to cities to work in factories. This meant that cities grew while smaller towns shrank and consolidated, which eliminates choices B, C, and D. Urban sprawl was a concept developed to describe a trend in the 20th century, not the Industrial Revolution of the late 18th and early 19th centuries.

11. **The correct answer is C.** A social movement is a group of people who organize themselves to work toward a goal they have to improve society. The goal or cause (choice A) itself cannot be the correct answer choice. Choices B, D, and E could be true of a group related to the social movement, but they are not true in all cases, making them incorrect choices.

12. **The correct answer is D.** Social mobility describes the process of individuals moving from one social class to another, as described in the question. Choices A and C relate to the development of identity within class and social groups, and choices B and E describe processes in the management of social class that are intended to produce different results than those described in the question.

13. **The correct answer is C.** Exogamy is a marriage outside of a community or group, which would NOT be allowed in a caste system that requires that individuals marry within their caste to preserve the existing social structure. Choice A (endogamy) would be allowed, and the other types of marriage (choices B, D, and E) do not include community or group status as a necessary component.

14. **The correct answer is E.** Conflict theory is in part derived from Karl Marx's theory that there is innate conflict between the working and ruling classes as they clash over limited resources and capital.

15. **The correct answer is D.** The "second shift" refers to the additional domestic and caregiving tasks performed by working parents. While the other choices relate to the difficulty many new families face in balancing economic needs with their role as parents, only choice D describes a caregiving task performed in addition to duties at work.

16. **The correct answer is D.** Bureaucracy is characterized by a hierarchical structure of unelected officials who impact government through formalized rules and procedures and a separation of labor through specialization. Because power is concentrated at the top of the organization in a hierarchical structure, not decentralized, choice D is the correct answer.

17. **The correct answer is C.** Conflict theory, developed by Karl Marx, posits that society is in a constant state of conflict because of the competition for limited resources, and this conflict creates systems of inequality—including schools—that are maintained by the groups with the most resources. Choice C does not reflect the view of conflict theory but is consistent with structural functionalism, which holds a more positive view of public education.

18. **The correct answer is C.** Countercultural movements seek to challenge the values, norms, and practices of the dominant culture. Choices A, B, and E are antithetical to counterculture, which defines itself in opposition to the dominant culture, and choice D is incorrect, as counterculture does require cultural expression.

19. **The correct answer is A.** Women disproportionately work in jobs that require more emotional labor, such as nursing, customer service, and teaching. This phenomenon is often linked to gender roles that women are expected to adopt, especially being perceived as more nurturing and emotionally attuned than men.

20. **The correct answer is B.** Credentialism is the term used to describe the overemphasis on credentials to qualify candidates for a job that does not require those credentials. While the other choices could be inferred as accurate about this situation, more information would be required.

21. **The correct answer is C.** Status inconsistency refers to when a person occupies multiple social positions with varying levels of prestige. While nurses are generally respected in society, nursing is one of the top pink-collar jobs, and someone adhering to feminist theory would likely point to the job's historical association with women to explain its relatively low pay. The other choices either reflect feminist theory unrelated to the given situation (choices B and D) or somewhat-related phenomena that would be cited by other schools of thought (choices A and E).

22. **The correct answer is E.** Prestige is the respect people give a certain profession. Professions that require more education and abstract thinking, while providing increased autonomy and pay, are given more prestige. The level of diversity within the occupation usually has little impact on prestige.

23. **The correct answer is A.** Double consciousness is a concept developed by W. E. B. Du Bois, a prominent sociologist famous for his ideas about race relations in the United States. The term describes the internal struggle African Americans face in trying to maintain connections to their identity and culture while navigating a society dominated by white culture.

24. **The correct answer is D.** An ecclesia is a religious organization that is formally connected to a government and has significant influence on the population which it helps oversee and shape. All of the other choices are not necessarily affiliated with a government and, thus, are incorrect.

25. **The correct answer is A.** Organic solidarity refers to social cohesion that is based on the interdependence of institutions in societies that do not rely on universal thinking to function. Durkheim sought to explore more complementary models of society in contrast to mechanical societies that rely on social homogeneity and repressive enforcement of shared norms.

26. **The correct answer is C.** Rapid population growth often leads to overcrowding in urban areas, which increases the demand for housing and stresses existing infrastructure such as public transportation and utility services. The other choices are either potential causes of rapid population growth (choices A and B) or do not represent logical outcomes from rapid population growth (choices D and E).

27. **The correct answer is C.** Socialization is the process through which people learn the norms of their culture. Assimilation (choice A) is the process through which a person from another culture learns the norms of a new culture through immersion. The other choices are unrelated to the process through which individuals acquire the norms of a culture.

28. **The correct answer is E.** Anomie is a situation in which there are few or no shared norms held collectively by society due to a breakdown in social order from a catastrophic event, war, or a severe conflict in systems of beliefs.

29. **The correct answer is C.** Structural mobility refers to changes in social hierarchy that change the opportunities available for different social groups, so the correct answer must involve a change at the structural or systemic level. Since the other options are largely individual, choice C is correct.

30. **The correct answer is E.** Symbolic interactionism focuses on the ways that the meanings of interactions between individuals are used to understand society. Choices A, B, C, and D all describe ways individuals communicate meaning through symbolic interactions. Since choice E describes how systems like law enforcement and punishment influence the behavior of an individual rather than how social interactions do, it is the answer NOT associated with symbolic interactionism.

31. **The correct answer is B.** Weber used the concept of *Verstehen* (which translates to *understanding* in English) to emphasize that sociologists need to understand the perspectives of the people they are studying in order to learn about them, rather than simply relying on data. Eric's desire to integrate interviews into his research to understand the perspectives of the people he is studying accomplishes this goal.

32. **The correct answer is D.** C. Wright Mills introduced the idea of the sociological imagination to address the responsibilities of the individual within society. He advocated for intellectuals to engage in public and political discourse rather than maintain a disinterested observation of public systems and processes.

33. **The correct answer is A.** A concept developed by Talcott Parsons, the sick role is used to describe the role within society of people who are physically or mentally ill or injured, including their rights, roles, and obligations. Ernesto's withdrawal from social and professional life, along with his focus on rest and recovery, are notable characteristics of the sick role.

34. **The correct answer is E.** Social capital is the information, connections, and privileges that help people leverage social networks. Choices A, B, and C are all broader concepts that apply to society as a whole, rather than on the individual level, and choice D describes the goal or process of increasing equity within society.

35. **The correct answer is C.** Symbolic interactionism is a microlevel theory because it focuses on interactions between individuals and groups of people. Each of the other choices relate to theories that deal with interactions at the societal level across much larger populations.

36. **The correct answer is C.** Conflict theory emphasizes the idea that competition for resources among different social classes will inevitably create conflict, and it is tied to the works of Karl Marx. Marx believed that the working class would eventually clash with the wealthy capitalists who held power in society despite contributing little to production of goods, a belief that mirrors the given scenario.

37. **The correct answer is C.** Medicalization is when a condition or behavior that was once considered a normal aspect of life becomes something that is seen as requiring medical intervention. While stigmatization (choice A) can certainly occur with the diagnosis of illness and the other choices represent various theories related to medical institutions, medicalization best fits this specific scenario.

38. **The correct answer is C.** Income polarization refers to the widening gap between the rich and poor within society. Choices A and E lead to a more equitable distribution of wealth, choice B leads to little relative change in wages across all levels, and choice D leads to more rigid divisions between social classes without increasing the gap between them.

39. **The correct answer is A.** Durkheim's perspective on deviance was that it is functional, normal, and universally present within societies. This countered the existing belief that deviance should be regarded as something disturbing, unwarranted, and infrequent.

40. **The correct answer is E.** Resocialization is the process through which people learn new norms, behaviors, and values. Resocialization often occurs during a significant life change such as a move or a change in primary social group. Mark living in the same neighborhood he grew up in would not be considered resocialization.

41. **The correct answer is A.** The "strength of weak ties," a phrase coined by Mark Granovetter, refers to social relationships that are not characterized by a close connection being beneficial in regard to employment. For example, a person's acquaintance from a previous job may help them get an interview for a new job.

42. **The correct answer is B.** A conflict theorist would posit that stratification is a product of one group exploiting another group to reap the benefit of limited resources, creating the roots of systemic social inequality and stratification between different social groups.

43. **The correct answer is E.** A secret society system is not a form of stratification. It refers to a group that is organized clandestinely and has secretive activities and membership, which do not necessarily afford members of that group special treatment or privileges that would relate to social stratification.

44. **The correct answer is D.** Within an experiment, the control group acts as an untreated research sample that can be used as a point of comparison for the groups who are subject to the intervention being implemented. In this case, the performance of the students who do not receive a beverage acts as the baseline to which Inga can compare the performance of the caffeinated students.

45. **The correct answer is C.** Max Weber believed that religion, specifically Calvinism, was the reason that capitalism developed in certain areas. This cemented the idea that religion played a crucial role in significant social change, influencing other institutions by allowing people to pursue their own interests.

46. **The correct answer is C.** A reference group is a group of people that an individual uses to understand their position in society relative to others. For example, someone who owns a condo might consider themselves well off compared with others in their neighborhood who rent apartments. However, compared with people in the suburbs who might own larger homes on lots of land, the same person might consider themselves less privileged.

47. **The correct answer is A.** Social control helps societies maintain social order by regulating individual behavior, discouraging deviant acts, and enforcing norms. Social sanctions (choice B) punish those who do not abide by the various rules of social control, while activism (choice C) and subcultures (choice E) serve to undermine social control. Collective effervescence (choice D) refers to rituals bringing groups together.

48. **The correct answer is C.** Alicia is facing informal negative sanctions through loss of reputation and shunning. There is no process or documentation associated with the sanctions, making it informal, which eliminates choices A and B. Positive sanctions (choices B and D) include celebration, positive social recognition, or praise, which Alicia did not receive. She has not broken any laws so there are no legal sanctions (choice E), though her actions would likely be considered distasteful by many people.

49. **The correct answer is B.** The Hawthorne effect is when study subjects behave differently because they are aware of being observed by a researcher. In this case, Cynthia might find that the visible camera influences the subjects' decisions about washing their hands, tainting her data and making it difficult for her to draw an accurate conclusion.

50. **The correct answer is E.** These achievements belong to Jane Addams, an iconic reformer during the Progressive Era of US politics and an important leader in the movement for women's suffrage. She was directly involved in the founding of sociology as a field in the United States through her association with members of the Chicago School of Sociology.

MY PRACTICE TEST SCORES BY CATEGORY		
Category	**Question Numbers**	**Raw Score**
Institutions	1, 8, 15, 16, 17, 24, 25, 33, 37, 38	_____ /10
Social patterns	2, 6, 7, 9, 10, 26	_____ /6
Social processes	3, 4, 11, 18, 27, 28, 39, 40, 41, 46, 47, 48	_____ /12
Social stratification	5, 12, 13, 19, 20, 21, 22, 29, 30, 34, 42, 43	_____ /12
The sociological perspective	14, 23, 31, 32, 35, 36, 44, 45, 49, 50	_____ /10
Total Raw Score		_____ /50
Full Test Raw Score Projection*		_____ /100

* Multiply total raw score by 2

Chapter 3

Diagnostic Test Answer Sheet

1. Ⓐ Ⓑ Ⓒ Ⓓ Ⓔ   10. Ⓐ Ⓑ Ⓒ Ⓓ Ⓔ   19. Ⓐ Ⓑ Ⓒ Ⓓ Ⓔ

2. Ⓐ Ⓑ Ⓒ Ⓓ Ⓔ   11. Ⓐ Ⓑ Ⓒ Ⓓ Ⓔ   20. Ⓐ Ⓑ Ⓒ Ⓓ Ⓔ

3. Ⓐ Ⓑ Ⓒ Ⓓ Ⓔ   12. Ⓐ Ⓑ Ⓒ Ⓓ Ⓔ   21. Ⓐ Ⓑ Ⓒ Ⓓ Ⓔ

4. Ⓐ Ⓑ Ⓒ Ⓓ Ⓔ   13. Ⓐ Ⓑ Ⓒ Ⓓ Ⓔ   22. Ⓐ Ⓑ Ⓒ Ⓓ Ⓔ

5. Ⓐ Ⓑ Ⓒ Ⓓ Ⓔ   14. Ⓐ Ⓑ Ⓒ Ⓓ Ⓔ   23. Ⓐ Ⓑ Ⓒ Ⓓ Ⓔ

6. Ⓐ Ⓑ Ⓒ Ⓓ Ⓔ   15. Ⓐ Ⓑ Ⓒ Ⓓ Ⓔ   24. Ⓐ Ⓑ Ⓒ Ⓓ Ⓔ

7. Ⓐ Ⓑ Ⓒ Ⓓ Ⓔ   16. Ⓐ Ⓑ Ⓒ Ⓓ Ⓔ   25. Ⓐ Ⓑ Ⓒ Ⓓ Ⓔ

8. Ⓐ Ⓑ Ⓒ Ⓓ Ⓔ   17. Ⓐ Ⓑ Ⓒ Ⓓ Ⓔ

9. Ⓐ Ⓑ Ⓒ Ⓓ Ⓔ   18. Ⓐ Ⓑ Ⓒ Ⓓ Ⓔ

Practice Test Answer Sheet

1. Ⓐ Ⓑ Ⓒ Ⓓ Ⓔ
2. Ⓐ Ⓑ Ⓒ Ⓓ Ⓔ
3. Ⓐ Ⓑ Ⓒ Ⓓ Ⓔ
4. Ⓐ Ⓑ Ⓒ Ⓓ Ⓔ
5. Ⓐ Ⓑ Ⓒ Ⓓ Ⓔ
6. Ⓐ Ⓑ Ⓒ Ⓓ Ⓔ
7. Ⓐ Ⓑ Ⓒ Ⓓ Ⓔ
8. Ⓐ Ⓑ Ⓒ Ⓓ Ⓔ
9. Ⓐ Ⓑ Ⓒ Ⓓ Ⓔ
10. Ⓐ Ⓑ Ⓒ Ⓓ Ⓔ
11. Ⓐ Ⓑ Ⓒ Ⓓ Ⓔ
12. Ⓐ Ⓑ Ⓒ Ⓓ Ⓔ
13. Ⓐ Ⓑ Ⓒ Ⓓ Ⓔ
14. Ⓐ Ⓑ Ⓒ Ⓓ Ⓔ
15. Ⓐ Ⓑ Ⓒ Ⓓ Ⓔ
16. Ⓐ Ⓑ Ⓒ Ⓓ Ⓔ
17. Ⓐ Ⓑ Ⓒ Ⓓ Ⓔ

18. Ⓐ Ⓑ Ⓒ Ⓓ Ⓔ
19. Ⓐ Ⓑ Ⓒ Ⓓ Ⓔ
20. Ⓐ Ⓑ Ⓒ Ⓓ Ⓔ
21. Ⓐ Ⓑ Ⓒ Ⓓ Ⓔ
22. Ⓐ Ⓑ Ⓒ Ⓓ Ⓔ
23. Ⓐ Ⓑ Ⓒ Ⓓ Ⓔ
24. Ⓐ Ⓑ Ⓒ Ⓓ Ⓔ
25. Ⓐ Ⓑ Ⓒ Ⓓ Ⓔ
26. Ⓐ Ⓑ Ⓒ Ⓓ Ⓔ
27. Ⓐ Ⓑ Ⓒ Ⓓ Ⓔ
28. Ⓐ Ⓑ Ⓒ Ⓓ Ⓔ
29. Ⓐ Ⓑ Ⓒ Ⓓ Ⓔ
30. Ⓐ Ⓑ Ⓒ Ⓓ Ⓔ
31. Ⓐ Ⓑ Ⓒ Ⓓ Ⓔ
32. Ⓐ Ⓑ Ⓒ Ⓓ Ⓔ
33. Ⓐ Ⓑ Ⓒ Ⓓ Ⓔ
34. Ⓐ Ⓑ Ⓒ Ⓓ Ⓔ

35. Ⓐ Ⓑ Ⓒ Ⓓ Ⓔ
36. Ⓐ Ⓑ Ⓒ Ⓓ Ⓔ
37. Ⓐ Ⓑ Ⓒ Ⓓ Ⓔ
38. Ⓐ Ⓑ Ⓒ Ⓓ Ⓔ
39. Ⓐ Ⓑ Ⓒ Ⓓ Ⓔ
40. Ⓐ Ⓑ Ⓒ Ⓓ Ⓔ
41. Ⓐ Ⓑ Ⓒ Ⓓ Ⓔ
42. Ⓐ Ⓑ Ⓒ Ⓓ Ⓔ
43. Ⓐ Ⓑ Ⓒ Ⓓ Ⓔ
44. Ⓐ Ⓑ Ⓒ Ⓓ Ⓔ
45. Ⓐ Ⓑ Ⓒ Ⓓ Ⓔ
46. Ⓐ Ⓑ Ⓒ Ⓓ Ⓔ
47. Ⓐ Ⓑ Ⓒ Ⓓ Ⓔ
48. Ⓐ Ⓑ Ⓒ Ⓓ Ⓔ
49. Ⓐ Ⓑ Ⓒ Ⓓ Ⓔ
50. Ⓐ Ⓑ Ⓒ Ⓓ Ⓔ

Printed in the USA
CPSIA information can be obtained
at www.ICGtesting.com
JSHW011058160124
55462JS00016B/132